POPE BENEDICT XVI

ALSO BY STEPHEN MANSFIELD

The Faith of the American Soldier

The Faith of George W. Bush

*Never Give In: The Extraordinary Character
of Winston Churchill*

Faithful Volunteers: The History of Religion in Tennessee

*Then Darkness Fled: The Liberating Philosophy
of Booker T. Washington*

*More Than Dates and Dead People:
Recovering a Christian View of History*

*Forgotten Founding Father: The Heroic Legacy
of George Whitefield*

POPE BENEDICT XVI

His Life and Mission

STEPHEN MANSFIELD

JEREMY P. TARCHER/PENGUIN

a member of Penguin Group (USA) Inc.

New York

JEREMY P. TARCHER/PENGUIN
Published by the Penguin Group
Penguin Group (USA) Inc., 375 Hudson Street, New York, New York 10014, USA •
Penguin Group (Canada), 90 Eglinton Avenue East, Suite 700, Toronto, Ontario
M4P 2Y3, Canada (a division of Pearson Penguin Canada Inc.) • Penguin Books Ltd,
80 Strand, London WC2R 0RL, England • Penguin Ireland, 25 St Stephen's Green,
Dublin 2, Ireland (a division of Penguin Books Ltd) • Penguin Group (Australia),
250 Camberwell Road, Camberwell, Victoria 3124, Australia • (a division of
Pearson Australia Group Pty Ltd) • Penguin Books India Pvt Ltd, 11 Community
Centre, Panchsheel Park, New Delhi–110 017, India • Penguin Group (NZ), Cnr
Airborne and Rosedale Roads, Albany, Auckland 1310, New Zealand (a division of
Pearson New Zealand Ltd) • Penguin Books (South Africa) (Pty) Ltd, 24 Sturdee
Avenue, Rosebank, Johannesburg 2196, South Africa

Penguin Books Ltd, Registered Offices: 80 Strand, London WC2R 0RL, England

An application has been submitted to register this book
with the Library of Congress.

ISBN 1-58542-450-1

Printed in the United States of America
1   3   5   7   9   10   8   6   4   2

Book design by Meighan Cavanaugh

Most Tarcher/Penguin books are available at special quantity discounts for bulk pur-
chase for sales promotions, premiums, fund-raising, and educational needs. Special
books or book excerpts also can be created to fit specific needs. For details, write
Penguin Group (USA) Inc. Special Markets, 375 Hudson Street, New York, NY 10014.

While the author has made every effort to provide accurate telephone numbers
and Internet addresses at the time of publication, neither the publisher nor the author
assumes any responsibility for errors, or for changes that occur after publication.
Further, the publisher does not have any control over and does not assume any
responsibility for author or third-party websites or their content.

To the Sisters of
St. Francis Hospital,
Columbus, Georgia

It often happens that I wake at night and begin to think about a serious problem and decide I must tell the Pope about it. Then I wake up completely and remember that I am the Pope.

POPE JOHN XXIII

CONTENTS

INTRODUCTION

"Please Don't Do This to Me!"

The year was 1968, and to the middle-aged theology professor it seemed that evil was spilling out into the world. The whole earth appeared to be in upheaval. The Soviets had invaded Czechoslovakia, the war in Vietnam raged on, and a leftist student uprising in France threatened to topple the Fifth Republic of Charles de Gaulle.

In America, Martin Luther King, Jr., and Robert Kennedy had been gunned down, and students enraged by their government's policies abroad took over college campuses and forced violent confrontations in the streets. The Beatles, who played Pied Piper to the young, had released an album called *Yellow Submarine* that seemed to summon their generation to a life of drugs and irrationality. It was a fearful, chaotic time for a man who was given to thought and order and system.

Still, the professor held his own. Though he had grown up in the rich Catholic traditions and idyllic beauty of Bavaria in southern Germany, he had wrestled with the meaning of truth through a Nazi seizure of power in his homeland, a calling to the priesthood, the earning of a doctorate in theology from the University of Munich and professorships at Bonn and Münster. He was no stranger to the clash of ideas. His students loved him for his unusual merging of gentleness and fierce intellectual hunger, for the way he urged them to seek out truth wherever it might be lurking. In fact, hadn't this professor been a theological expert at Vatican II some years before? Wasn't he a progressive who had then called the Church to a greater openness and accommodation of the modern world? In truth, it was just this spirit of inquiry and willingness to embrace the new that caused eager students to flood into his courses.

Yet things were changing—and often in an ugly, disorienting way. Just the year before, in 1967, the professor had been part of the celebration of the 150th anniversary of the Faculty for Catholic Theology at Tübingen, the university where he now taught. They had done it "old style," with liturgy, Latin, and high ceremony befitting the occasion. It had been a glorious moment and the professor didn't mind so much that the pageantry concealed tensions among the faculty over the ultimate nature of truth and what it meant for theology. The ideas of those like Rudolph Bultmann and Martin Heidegger—existentialist philosophers who asked whether all truth was relative—were widely discussed. Even though the professor believed that the thinking of these men drained Christian theology of its historic content, he still understood that such new ideas must be considered in the context of learned debate. So, he had enjoyed the anniversary festivities and looked forward to the sounding trumpets of theological battle.

It was not long, though, before existentialism gave way to a darker force on the Tübingen campus: Marxism. As the professor later wrote, "The Marxist revolution kindled the whole university with its fervor, shaking it to its very foundations."[1] In the Marxist worldview, faith is frequently trumped by atheism, the church is replaced by the state, community by the political party, and man as a spirit is replaced by man as an economic unit. When many students at Tübingen embraced this secular religion and rejected the old order, the school became a "battle zone."[2]

"It was horrible," the dean of the Catholic theological faculty later remembered. "The university was in chaos. Students kept professors from talking. They were verbally abusive, very primitive and aggressive . . ."[3]

It was all a shock to the professor's soul. On one occasion, students crashed into a meeting of the faculty senate and took over. On another, a classroom discussion erupted into a furniture-throwing fight. Anger and rebellion were thick throughout the school. Many of the young whom the professor had learned to love became long-haired, unkempt radicals who were insulting, arrogant, and threatening. It was a sad and fearful time.

Yet the professor was trained to look beyond the immediate to the long-term meaning of ideas. When he did so, he grew even more disturbed by what was happening at Tübingen. First, he had expected prudence from the theology faculty, had hoped that the men of God who taught truth would "represent a bulwark against the Marxist temptation." It was not to be. "Now the opposite was the case: they became its real ideological center." It was horrible for the professor to watch and made him fear for the future of the faith. He was also fearful over what was happening to theology. These new radicals retained biblical language but gave the words a new political meaning. Now, "sin" frequently meant "oppression," "redemption" meant "revolution," and "righteousness" meant "social justice," as defined by Marxist ideology. The professor realized that if you alter Christian language, you lose Christian meaning and, ultimately, lose God in the process.[4]

This, the professor felt, would mean finally, "The party takes the place of God." Now he understood: Marxism was not a new ideology by which to interpret Christianity, Marxism was a replacement for Christianity—a dark, sinister, secular reworking of the very truth of God. As the professor later wrote, "I have seen the frightful face of this atheistic piety unveiled, its psychological terror, the abandon with which every moral consideration could be thrown overboard as bourgeois residue when the ideological goal was at stake."[5]

These months of Marxist upheaval at Tübingen were torturous for the professor. Faculty members ceased speaking to one another. Students whom the professor had counseled over coffee now regarded him as a relic of an old and oppressive system. Worse, the faith he so cherished was now trampled underfoot by the very students he hoped would be its ambassadors.

In desperation, the professor joined with other like-minded Catholics to build alliances across denominational lines. There were Protestants, most of them Lutherans, who were willing to stand with their Catholic friends against the Marxist tide. Now, theological disputes between believing Christians seemed frivolous. The professor recognized that anti-Marxist followers of Jesus were "in the same boat," that their differences were "small indeed in the face of the challenge we now confronted, which put us in a position of having, together, to bear witness to our common faith in the living God and in Christ, the incarnate Word."[6]

So they stood together and they gave witness to their faith and, in time, the crisis passed. But the professor never forgot. He would always remember those days at Tübingen: how quickly professed Christians conformed to worldly thinking, what a powerful force ideas could be, and how chaos ensued when the foundations of faith were undermined. He would forever be haunted by the vision of angry students, eager to overthrow the proven faith of centuries to reach for the passing ideological fancies of this age.

No, he would never forget. Not when he left Tübingen to become a professor at Regensburg. Not when he became a cardinal or was made the archbishop of Munich. Nor did he forget when he was appointed by Pope John Paul II to head the Congregation for the Doctrine of the Faith (CDF), where it would be his job to assure the purity of the Church's teaching, to be, in effect, the earthly bodyguard of the truth of God. And he did not forget on April 19, 2005, when this professor, whose name was Joseph Ratzinger, became Benedict XVI, the 265th pontiff of the Roman Catholic Church.

He was supposed to be the Grand Inquisitor of a new generation, the Torquemada of our time: a man who hunted down heretics, crushed rebellion, and devastated lives all in the name of Jesus Christ. His critics called him "the Enforcer," God's Rottweiler," and even "the Panzer Cardinal," an insulting allusion to his brief stint in the

Hitler Youth and his allegedly tanklike tactics. His Congregation for the Doctrine of the Faith was referred to as "God's Gestapo" and the "Headquarters of the Thought Police."

When he was elected pope, conservative Catholics rejoiced but those who had despised him as a "heresy hunter" sent up a great wail of anguish. An angered priest promised on network television to organize prayer for Benedict XVI to have a short reign. The leading Italian newspaper, *Corriere della Serra*, carried a cartoon that alluded to John Paul II's now famous introduction as pope from the balcony of St. Peter's Basilica in October 1978. "I do not know whether I can express myself in your—in our—Italian language. If I make mistakes," he added with a winning smile, "you will correct me." The cartoon showed Benedict at the same balcony looking out at the crowds and warning, "And if I make a mistake, woe to you if you correct me!"

Other newspaper headlines told the tale. The Dutch daily, *Algemeen Dagblad*, sported a front page headline that read "From Hitler Youth to Holy See." Italy's *La Repubblica* proclaimed Benedict "A Warrior to Challenge Modernity." France's left-wing *Libération* titled its editorial on the new pope "Intransigence." And a headline placed over an Associated Press story that circulated on the Internet was shamefully titled "Nazi Pope Elected."

American news networks reminded their viewers that it had been Joseph Ratzinger who issued the statement that many took as a condemnation of the liberal Catholicism of presidential candidate John Kerry. In June of 2004, the Congregation for the Doctrine of the Faith, under Ratzinger's direction, issued a letter calling abortion "a grave sin" and insisting that the sacrament of Holy Eucharist should be denied in "the case of a Catholic politician consistently campaigning and voting for permissive abortion and euthanasia laws."[7] A majority of Catholic voters supported Kerry's opponent, George W. Bush, and many Ratzinger critics expressed their resentment of Vatican intrusion into American politics.[8] That the instigator of this intrusion was now pope only increased their ire.

Clearly, many saw Joseph Ratzinger as the archetype of the sin-sniffing, legalistic, cold-hearted religious bureaucrat. And now he was the pope.

Yet as time passed after his election, and his supporters acquired the media spotlight, a new image of the man who became Benedict XVI began to emerge. It turned out that Joseph Ratzinger was by most accounts a man with a gentle manner, a quick mind, and a deep soul. He even had a sense of humor, like John Paul before him, who once told an Italian muscle man, "If I wasn't wearing this dress, I could whip you."

Ratzinger's simplicity was legend in Rome. For twenty-three years he had set off each morning on foot from his apartment along the Piazza della Città Leonina, just above the last stop of the No. 64 bus, adorned in simple cassock and blending in among the flocks of priests who poured through the streets of Vatican City. As he made his way past carts filled with Vatican souvenirs, he was often stopped by tourists needing directions who had no idea who he was. His command of language served him well as he kindly told a French visitor the way to the Sala Stampa or explained to an American family when the pope would make his next public appearance. Finally, he would reach the CDF in the Piazza Sant'Uffizio promptly at 9:00 a.m. and begin work in his well-ordered but unimpressive office. It did not seem the kind of place where a torturer of heretics might ply his trade.

In fact, the world soon learned that he had prayed he

would not have to be pope. A man of bookish ways, he had hoped to return to the academic life when John Paul II died and his service at the CDF automatically came to an end. It was not to be. The cardinals of the conclave quickly set their sights on Ratzinger and when he realized what might happen, that he could be elected pope, he quietly pleaded with his God, "Please don't do this to me." Later he told some German pilgrims, "Evidently, this time He didn't listen to me."[9]

The world also learned that on the day Pope Benedict was elected, he invited the cardinals of the conclave to join him for dinner. The menu was soup, veal cordon bleu, and ice cream for dessert. The leaders of the world's 1.1 billion Catholics then toasted the new pope with glasses of Asti Spumante. It turned out that the ice cream and the Asti Spumante were Pope Benedict's idea. Human touches like these had long been endearing this man to the faithful. There was even a Cardinal Ratzinger Fan Club with a Web site that sold paraphernalia sporting the slogan "Putting the smackdown on heresy since 1981."

It also did not escape notice that the choice of Ratzinger for pope was hailed by many outside the Roman Catholic communion. Charles Colson, a member of America's largest Protestant denomination, the Southern Baptists, declared that "faithful Christians ought to be thrilled" with the choice for the next pope. Colson, and other non-Catholics as diverse as T. D. Jakes and the Archbishop of Canterbury, celebrated Ratzinger's opposition to the "culture of death" in the world and his focus on the sacrifice of Jesus as the solution for mankind. It was not the kind of response many Catholics expected from their Protestant brethren, particularly from denominations that had at one time in their history deemed the papacy as the seat of the Antichrist.

There were also the words of one of Ratzinger's Tübingen colleagues, a Professor Max Seckler, who recounted for the *New York Times* that the theology and tactics of the CDF had not necessarily reflected the personal views of the man who was now pope. As Seckler remembered, "Once, about ten years ago when I was visiting him [Ratzinger] in Rome, he told me, 'I have my personal sense of freedom, my sympathy for freedom. I have to keep it to myself. I have to obey the pope [John Paul II]. The pope told me that it is my biggest obligation not to have my own opinions.'"[10]

Clearly, if Ratzinger is not the caricature of the Grand

Inquisitor—the dark-souled cleric who wrings confessions from victims on the rack—and if his more than twenty years at the CDF do not necessarily reveal his own ideas, then the question of who he really is and how he will lead as pope is still open. Will he make it his central task to hunt down dissidents or will he seek to evangelize Europe and heal the breaches with other Christian communions, as he has said? Will he become the pastor and poet that his predecessor was, or will he assume the manner of "theologian-in-chief," as some fear? Was he chosen by the cardinals because he is conservative, unassuming, and old—assuring a papacy that is short and uneventful but one that shifts the limelight from the papacy to the episcopacy, to the cardinals and the bishops, in a manner that was impossible during the reign of "John Paul Superstar"? Or is there something unique about this man that the electing cardinals know and that the world outside the Vatican is soon to find out?

In a papacy that is still being born, we can discover the beginnings of our answers—and new questions with them—by looking back at the life journey of Joseph Ratzinger. His story, his words, his beliefs, and the nature of his closest associates are the surest key to understanding who this man is and how he will lead in the time his God allows him. This is no small matter. The reign of Pope Benedict begins at a time when his Church faces enormous challenges and divisions, when religious faith of all kinds is surging to new influence, and when, thanks to his predecessor, his followers will expect an outspoken, activist leader who is more than a caretaker, more than merely a custodian in the John Paul II museum. So it is that this book, an attempt at a first draft of history, is an effort to discern Pope Benedict's response to the question that all popes have had to answer since the Apostle Peter tried to escape persecution by leaving Rome and was confronted by his Lord's question, "Quo vadis?"—"Which way are you going?"

ONE

Bavaria: Years of Worship and War

His name was Boniface and he is known to history as the Apostle of Germany. Though he lived some twelve hundred years before Joseph Ratzinger was born, he is vital to the life of the man who would become the first pope elected in the twenty-first century. He was the pioneering spirit who planted the Christian faith in Germany and who first planted the traditions of the Church so deeply in the spiritually fertile Bavarian soil. The legends that his deeds inspired gave the world many of the traditions now associated with Christmas: the Christmas tree, the Yule log, and the Advent wreath. So revered was his memory that even the Protestant reformer Martin Luther retained the symbol of the Christmas tree in honor of the great man's "conquering of Germany for Christ."

Yet the memory of Boniface is essential to the Joseph Ratzinger story for perhaps a deeper reason. As a boy, Joseph grew up in the environs of a church first established through the evangelical work of Boniface. The legends of this great man would have filled his early imagination, would have framed his childhood dreams the way all young boy's heroes define what they one day hope to be. It is more than likely that the example of the Apostle to the Germans inspired Ratzinger to serve his nation and his church. It is not surprising, then, that Ratzinger mentions Boniface in the very first paragraph of *Milestones*, the autobiography he published in 1998, acknowledging that his hero "gave the whole of what was then Bavaria its ecclesial structure."

The figure that—more than any other individual—Christianized the early Germanic lands actually spent his first forty years of life in quiet service to the church near his native home in Exeter, England. He discipled young converts, cared for the sick, and administered relief for the poor. He was a gifted scholar as well, expounding Bible doctrine for a small theological center and compiling the first Latin grammar written in England. But in AD 718, Boniface left the comfort and security of this life to become a missionary to the savage Teutonic tribes of Germany.

Wherever he went among the fierce Norsemen who had settled along the Danish and German coast, he was forced to face the awful specter of their brutal pagan practices—which included human mutilation and vestal sacrifice. When he arrived in the region of Hesse, Boniface decided to strike at the root of such superstitions. He publicly announced that he would destroy their gods. He then marched toward their great sacred grove. The awestruck crowd at Geismar followed along and then watched as he cut down the sacred Oak of Thor, an ancient object of pagan worship standing atop the summit of Mount Gudenberg near Fritzlar. The pagans, who had expected immediate judgment against such sacrilege, were forced to acknowledge that their gods were powerless to protect their own sanctuaries. Together, they professed faith in Christ.

Not long after, a young boy who had heard of Boniface's boldness rushed into his camp. He breathlessly told of a sacrifice that was to be offered that very evening—his sister was to serve as the vestal virgin. Hurrying through the snowy woods and across the rough terrain, Boniface and the boy arrived at the dense sacred grove just in time to see the Druid priest raise his knife into the darkened air. But as the blade plunged downward Boniface hurtled toward the horrid scene. He had nothing in his hands save a small wooden cross. Lunging forward, he reached the girl just in time to see the blade of the knife pierce the cross—thus saving her life.

The Druid priest toppled back. The worshippers were astonished. There was a brief moment of complete silence. Boniface seized upon it. He proclaimed the Gospel to them then and there, declaring that the ultimate sacrifice had already been made by Christ on the cross at Golgotha—there was no need for others.

Captivated by the bizarre scene before them, the small crowd listened intently to his words. After explaining to them the once-and-for-all provision of the Gospel, he turned toward the sacred grove. With the sacrificial knife in hand, he began hacking off low hanging branches. Passing them around the circle, he told each family to take the small fir boughs home as a reminder of the completeness of Christ's work on the tree of Calvary. They were to adorn their hearths with the tokens of His grace. They might even chop great logs from the grove as fuel for their home fires, he suggested—not so much to herald the destruction of their pagan ways but rather to memorialize the provision of Christ's coming. Upon these things they were to meditate over the course of the next four weeks, until the great celebration of Christmas.

Such exploits inspired a number of Advent traditions. The Advent wreath—a fir garland set with five candles, one for each Sunday in Advent and one for Christmas Day—was quickly established as a means of reenacting the Gospel lesson of Boniface. In addition, the Christmas tree, decorated with candles and tinsel, strings of lights and garlands under the eaves and across the mantels, and the Yule log burning in the fireplace were favorite reminders of the season's essential message.

In time, Boniface established a number of thriving parishes. He eventually became a mentor and support to the Carolingians, and he reformed the Frankish Church, which Charles Martel had plundered just a few years before. Ultimately, he discipled Pepin the Short, the father of Charlemagne.

Then, when he was over seventy, Boniface resigned his pastoral responsibilities, in order to spend his last years working among the fierce Frieslanders. With a small company, he successfully reached large numbers in the previously unevangelized area in the northeastern Germanic territories. On Whitsun Eve, Boniface and his aide, Eoban, were preparing for the baptism of some of the new converts at Dokkum, along the frontier of the Netherlands. Boniface had been quietly reading in his tent while awaiting the arrival of his new converts when a hostile band of pagan warriors descended on the camp. He would not allow his companions to defend him. As he was exhorting them to trust in God and to welcome the prospect of dying for the faith, they were attacked—and Boniface was one of the first to fall.

Though his voice was stilled that day, his testimony grew only louder, surer, and bolder. And thus, to this day, his message and his legend endure—both in the traditions of Advent and in the life and work of his latter-day spiritual son, Joseph Ratzinger. Like Boniface, Ratzinger left behind a life of scholarship to spread the message of his Church. Like Boniface, he has served as an archbishop in Germany. And, like his hero, he now seeks to reclaim

Europe from a resurgence of the very pagan faiths that Boniface battled in his day.

～⁂～

Joseph Ratzinger was born in a manner that presaged much of what he would become. He arrived in the world at 4:15 a.m. on the eve of Easter, Holy Saturday, to parents named Joseph and Mary. The date was April 16, 1927, a day so cold that the child's older brother and sister, Georg and Mary, were not allowed to attend his baptism for fear of catching cold. It was an absence they regretted all their lives. Young Joseph was baptized with water newly blessed for the Easter celebration, a fact that grew in symbolism throughout his life.

As he later wrote in his autobiography,

To be the first person baptized with the new water was seen as a significant act of Providence. I have always been filled with thanksgiving for having had my life immersed in this way in the Easter mystery, since this could only be a sign of blessing. To be sure it was not Easter Sunday but Holy Saturday, but, the more I reflect on it, the more this seems to be fitting for the nature of our human life: we are still awaiting Easter; we are not yet standing in the full light but walking toward it full of trust.

At his birth, his family lived in a small Bavarian town call Marktl am Inn, in a lush region of rivers fed by mountain snows, towering and mysterious forests, and beautifully situated highland lakes. In the landscape of his later memory he recalled a replica of Louis XIV's Palace of Versailles and a shrine to Mary at Altotting that drew streams of pilgrims. Though his family would move by the time he was two and then move again three more times during his youth, the sensual landscape of Bavaria reached to him wherever he lived and filled both his senses and his memory all his days.

In a 1981 essay on the Feast of Corpus Christi, Ratzinger extolled the gentle merging of religion, nature, and village custom that formed the backdrop to his early life:

I can still smell those carpets of flowers and the freshness of the birch trees; I can see all the houses decorated, the banners, the singing; I can still hear the village band, which indeed sometimes dared more, on this occasion, than it was able. I remember the joie de vivre of the local lads, firing their gun salutes—which was their way of welcoming Christ as a head of state, *the* Head of State, the Lord of the world, present on their streets and in their village. On this day people celebrated the perpetual presence of Christ as if it were a state visit in which not even the smallest village was neglected.[1]

The deeply pious brand of Bavarian Catholicism that Ratzinger knew in his youth moved liturgy out of the church and into the lives of the people. On holy days, village life became liturgy. There were symbols and rituals and processions all designed to celebrate and welcome the risen Christ. This sense of the holy community never left Ratzinger and formed the defining vision of his life: the people of God in a setting of beauty, physically living out the rituals of faith in their homes and hamlets. It is a theme that surfaces time and again in his writing and his preaching. When his biography was presented to the German-speaking world at a press conference in a Bavarian monastery, the man who introduced Cardinal Ratzinger said, "You have always made it clear that heaven and earth are bound together in a special way in Bavaria."

It may be that faith and village life were so dear to Ratzinger in his youth because the outer world was so fearful. He was born when Germany was still suffering the aftermath of World War I. Though the war had been caused by a tragic combination of entangling alliances and overheated nationalism, Germany alone was blamed at the peace conference that finally ended the conflict. Forced to pay war reparations, Germany descended into economic devastation. Unemployment was rampant, food prices soared, and currency became worthless. It would be on the wings of a nation's bitterness over such conditions that a disheveled Austrian housepainter named Adolf Hitler would rise to power.

Still, Ratzinger's early world was a haven from such concerns for a time. His parents were deeply religious and made sure that the home was filled with symbols of faith, with hymns and with family devotion. His father was a policeman and the family often lived above the police station, frequently on the town square. In some respects, his early life seems nearly idyllic. He acquired a love of reading from his parents and spent many a day against a shady tree lost in literature. His passion for music grew naturally from the richly musical Bavarian culture and from his own family's love of singing. He spent hours playing Beethoven and Brahms on the piano, but Mozart was his muse. In later life, he once said of Mozart's music, "It is so luminous and yet at the same time so deep. It contains the whole tragedy of human existence."

He was a bookish boy and fared poorly at sports. Still, he loved hiking the nearby mountains, often with his mother, and reveled in games with other children along the banks of rivers or the precipices of mountains. Always, the land reached for him and seems to have somehow nurtured his soul. Writing of a hike to a wooded chapel with his mother, Ratzinger recalled, "We three children would often make a little pilgrimage with our dear mother to this spot and allow the peace of the place to have its effect on us." Again, recalling the village and countryside of one of his boyhood homes, he wrote that Tittmoning "remains my childhood's land of dreams."

Of all his early influences, though, it was clearly the Church and the religious dramas of Bavarian culture that most shaped him. He was a sensitive, intelligent child upon whom the grand liturgies that gave time its rhythm had deep effect. When the liturgy of the angels was celebrated in a darkened church lit only by candles, young Joseph's heart permanently captured both the visual image and the sense of holy mystery that permeated the affair. When the gloom of winter was broken simply by stepping from a frigid night into a warm church brilliantly decorated for Christmas, it left a lasting and tender impression. And when, on Easter morning, the blackened windows of the church were suddenly opened to the brilliant morning light upon the pastor singing "Christ is Risen!"—Joseph remembered and he understood. These images became the pillars of his inner temple of faith.

Moreover, they served to frame his worldview. He later wrote in his autobiography,

> I could not dream of anything more beautiful. It was a riveting adventure to move by degrees into the mysterious world of the liturgy, which was being enacted before us and for us there on the altar. It was becoming more and more clear to me that here I was encountering a reality that no one had simply thought up, a reality that no official authority or great individual had created. It bore the whole weight of history within itself, and yet, at the same time, it was much more than the product of human history.

It may have been just this inspiration through liturgy that prepared young Joseph for the moment he would decide to be a priest. On a sun-drenched spring day in 1932, when Joseph was five, a black limousine swept into the square of his village. Inside was Michael Cardinal von Faulhaber, the archbishop of Munich, who was visiting the outer reaches of his archdiocese. "Resplendent in his princely robes," the archbishop stepped out of his car to a welcome of adoring children. Joseph was among them, and was smitten by the spectacle.

As his older brother, Georg, later recalled, "He came home and told our father that night, 'I want to be a cardinal.' It wasn't so much the car, since we weren't technically minded. It was the way the cardinal looked, his bearing and the garments he was wearing, that made such an impression on him."[2] As unlikely as it may seem, young Joseph's life never wavered from the dream of the priesthood from that moment on.

Perhaps as important as the impression of a cardinal on a young boy's mind is the fact that the event took place in 1932. Already that year, Adolf Hitler's National Socialists had become the largest party in the German Reichstag with 230 seats. By the end of January the following year, an aged President Hindenburg would name Hitler the chancellor of the Reich. The time of sorrows had begun.

When later generations are tempted to believe that all Germans bought into the Nazi lies and that Catholics were the worst of all, they should remember men like Joseph Ratzinger, Sr. Though he was a policeman, a minor government official, who might have held his tongue to protect his job, he instead spoke publicly at town meetings against the violence and atheism of the Nazi movement. "Our father was a bitter enemy of Nazism," Georg Ratzinger remembered, "because he believed it was in conflict with our faith. That was the example he set for us."

The courage of the elder Ratzinger knew no bounds. He spoke to all who would listen about the evils of Adolf Hitler and his Brownshirts and thought nothing of confronting Nazi officials with the error of their ways. His passion was fueled by his faith and by the threat he believed atheistic Nazism was to the deeply pious lives of the German—particularly the Bavarian—people. "My father," the younger Joseph Ratzinger later remembered, "was one who with unfailing clairvoyance saw that a victory of Hitler's would not be a victory for Germany but rather a victory of the Antichrist that would surely usher in apocalyptic times for all believers, and not only for them."

Despite his prophetic views, though, the elder Joseph was required to watch in silence as his children were sucked into the Nazi orbit. On the day that President Hindenburg named Hitler Germany's chancellor, the two older Ratzinger children were forced to tramp through their village in a pouring rain as part of a celebratory parade. Those in the village who had been secret Nazi spies now donned their brown uniforms openly, inspiring terror among their neighbors. The Ratzinger children were required to join the Hitler Youth or the League of German Girls. Though all able-bodied Aryan youth were required to attend, it was a blow to the sensibilities of the Ratzinger family. The two parents were pressured to inform on priests who were deemed "enemies of the Reich." As the younger Joseph later proudly declared, "It goes without saying that my father had no part in this. On the contrary, he would warn and aid priests he knew were in danger."

Beyond these indoctrinations, the rise of Nazism in Germany in the 1930s brought little immediate change to the Ratzingers' lives or the life of their village. For years things progressed much as they had before Hitler's ascendancy. The few attempts at bringing the adult locals in line with the Reich's protoreligious ideology tended to fail miserably. On one occasion, a schoolteacher who was enthusiastic about Nazi ideology constructed a maypole that was intended to restore pagan Germanic religion and gradually expel Christianity. The villagers, though, appeared more interested in the sausages that hung upon the pole than in any change in their historic Christian ways.

It was about this time that the Ratzingers moved just outside of a city called Traunstein, where ten-year-old Joseph began attending a "humanistic gymnasium," a kind of advanced junior high school for the study of classical languages. It would prove to be a time of intellectual awakening. Joseph gave further evidence of what his earlier schooling had already revealed: he was brilliant, particularly in the study of Greek and Latin. In fact, there is a sense that the study of ancient languages saved him and this may explain why, even late in his life, long after Vatican II had removed Latin as the official language of the Catholic Mass, Joseph Ratzinger still believed at least some of the Mass ought to be said in Latin. "In retrospect," he later wrote, "it seems to me that an education in Greek and Latin antiquity created a mental attitude that resisted seduction by a totalitarian ideology." Joseph discovered what many throughout history have also learned: a well-educated mind is a bulwark against every form of human tyranny.

Not only was the study of classical languages of benefit in resisting Nazism, but some of Joseph's teachers who were devout Catholics changed the official curriculum to weed out vestiges of the destructive Nazi ideology. One music teacher crossed out the phrase *Juda den Tod* (to Judah death) in a song and wrote instead *Wende die Not* (dispel our plight). Others took the meager amount of biblical instruction that was allowed, expanded it, and made sure their students knew that the Bible stood opposed to Hitler's atheism and anti-Semitism.

After several years of gymnasium, Joseph was urged by his pastor to attend a minor seminary called St. Michael's, which was something like a religious high school intended to integrate youth into spiritual callings. His parents agreed and in 1939—the same year that Hitler's troops invaded Poland—he not only entered a new course of study but found himself living for the first time in a boarding school. It was not an easy transition. Discipline at the school was rigid, with every minute of the day regimented according to a strict schedule of study and exercise. He was also younger than most of the other boys, and it only added to his athletic insecurities that he was years behind his teammates in football or rugby. The other boys were gracious, though, and realized that Joseph's real gifts were of mind, if not of body. Their friendship began to pull him out of himself and teach him what it meant to have comrades. "I had to learn how to fit into the group," he later wrote, "how to come out of my solitary ways and start building a community with others by giving and receiving. For this experience I am very grateful because it was important for my subsequent life."

It was during the next few years that life in Germany took its darkest turn. In 1940, Nazi troops occupied Denmark, Norway, Holland, Belgium, Luxembourg, and France. In 1941, Hitler decided to invade the Soviet Union on a front that reached from the North Pole to the Black Sea. Joseph was on a class outing when the news reached him and though he was only fourteen, he realized that this extension of the war "could only take a turn for the worse." He and his classmates "thought of Napoleon; we thought of Russia's immeasurable distances where somewhere the German attack had to run aground."

These schoolchildren were right, as time would disastrously reveal.

Amid the cloud of war, Joseph's life began to change rapidly. Troops arrived in his home village in huge transports, some of them horribly wounded, and homes were quickly commandeered as headquarters or hospitals. News soon came that some of Joseph's childhood friends had been killed at the front. This only made Georg's departure for the army more fearful. In 1942, he was drafted into the Reichsarbeitsdienst (work service of the Reich) and made a radio operator in the signal corps. He would experience tours of duty in France, Holland, and Czechoslovakia before serving at the Italian front in 1944. There, he would be wounded and returned to convalesce at the same seminary in Traunstein that his younger brother, Joseph, attended. Once Georg regained his strength, though, he was returned to the Italian front, where the Ratzinger family lost contact with him.

Oddly, Joseph's life during these years took an inward turn. While Europe suffered from the godless ambitions of his nation's leader, Joseph lived a simple life at the minor seminary in Traunstein where he grew in both mind and spirit. He reveled in his love of classical languages and added to them the study of mathematics. Then he discovered literature and read by the hour the works of great Germans like Goethe, Schiller, Eichendorff, Mörike, Stifter, Raabe, and Kleist. It was also a season of growth in his faith. "This was a time of interior exaltation," he remembered, "full of hope for the great things that were gradually opening up to me in the boundless realm of the spirit."

Soon, earthly concerns intruded. In 1943, the Reich determined that all youths attending boarding schools should be drafted into the antiaircraft defense (Flak). The intention was to allow the students to continue their studies while training them to help defend against enemy aircraft. Along with his other seminarians, Joseph was trundled off to the Flak in Munich, where he learned how to spot enemy aircraft and continued his studies at the famous Maximiliansgymnasium.

His time in the Flak was the beginning of a truly unusual military career. He never learned to fire a gun. In fact, his weapons were never loaded. This was true even when his unit was assigned to guard a branch of the Bavarian Motor Works (BMW) to the north of Munich. He would spend his days in uniform moving from place to place with the lightest military responsibilities, but he would be witness to horrors that would never leave him. At the BMW plant, he saw laborers conscripted from a branch of the Dachau concentration camp and witnessed Hungarian Jews being shipped to their deaths.

Still, his time in the Flak often gave him privacy and time for spiritual development he could not have expected. When his unit was assigned to Gilching, he and his comrades were exempted from military exercise, each had his own private quarters, and there was even time for the active Catholics to organize religious instruction and occasionally visit churches. This was largely due to the efforts of a particularly irascible noncommissioned officer who defended the autonomy of the unit "tooth and nail." Joseph remembered these months as a season of "independent living." He also remembers how the German people began to look to the Allied invasion as deliverance.

When he had reached military age and was released from the Flak, Joseph returned home on September 10, 1944, to find his draft notice awaiting him on the family's kitchen table. It was a horrible time to enter the German army. The scent of defeat already filled the land and conditions for soldiers were desperate. Joseph found himself

stationed at a camp where three countries intersect—
Austria, Czechoslovakia, and Hungary. He became part of
a labor detail ruled by the so-called Austrian Legion, a
band of old Nazis, some of whom had done time in prison.
They were ideologues and tyrants. Joseph escaped the
worst of the abuse because he had already admitted publicly that he intended to be a Catholic priest. This kept
him out of the SS but also made him the butt of countless
religious insults.

His war career continued to go oddly. He was kept in
the field as part of the labor detail but never sent to the
front, which drew ever closer. On November 20, 1944, he
was sent home, presumably to wait for a call to join a forward unit. It never came. Then he was ordered to Munich,
where he was placed under the command of an officer
who hated the war, hated Hitler even more, and cared
compassionately for his troops. There seemed to be little
to do, though, and Joseph passed the Christmas of 1944
away from home and in a depressing barracks among
homesick, disillusioned men.

During January of 1945, Joseph's unit was moved from
place to place, seemingly without purpose. The depres-
sion of the men deepened and when Hitler died not long

after, Joseph decided it was time to go home. Without much planning or fanfare, he simply deserted. He made his way along a quiet back road toward Traunstein and was almost home safely when two guards appeared and ordered him to halt. Fortunately, these two men were as war-weary as Joseph was. When they saw that his arm was in a sling due to a slight injury, they said, "Comrade, you are wounded. Move on!" Joseph did and shortly returned to his family home unhurt.

Now, there were new challenges. The Ratzinger home had been made into a kind of boardinghouse and in addition to two nuns, there was also a sergeant major from the German air force under its roof. Joseph worried that he might be found out as a deserter, for he was surely of fighting age, but his father kept the sergeant major so busy arguing about the failures of the Reich that the man barely had time to notice him.

Finally, the Americans arrived in Traunstein and chose the Ratzinger's house as their headquarters. Joseph, identified as a soldier, was marched off to a prisoner of war camp nearby in Ulm. Before leaving, though, he shoved pencils and a notebook into his pack, which allowed him to sketch and write verse during the long hours of his imprisonment. On June 19, 1945, he was released from the American prison and returned home. Hitching a ride on a dairy truck, he arrived home long before he had expected to and saw his hometown at a moment that etched itself in his memory. It was sunset and there was music coming from the church, since it was the evening of the Feast of the Sacred Heart of Jesus. As Joseph later recalled, "The heavenly Jerusalem itself could not have appeared more beautiful to me at that moment."

Now the family was united—all except for Georg. No one had heard from him for many weeks. There was an air of nervous anticipation that hung over the home. Was Georg even alive? It was a question no one dared to voice but all pondered. Then, on a hot July day, he appeared, darkly tanned from the Italian sun. The Ratzingers did as many German families did in those days when loved ones survived unexpectedly the bloodshed of war: they gathered around the family piano and lifted their voices to their God. "Holy God we praise thy name," they sang and held each other in gratitude that the dark Nazi night had passed.

TWO

Priest and Professor:
Contending for the Faith

I t is a tale of two men. Both are numbered among the most brilliant and influential thinkers of all time. Both rose from obscurity to launch movements that changed the course of civilizations. Both transcended their quiet, contemplative, and pious lifestyles to become champions of stunning intellectual and social reform. And both are considered among the greatest of the saints of the Church.

Yet only one of these men became the most profound intellectual influence on the life of Joseph Ratzinger. Only one was the thinker that Pope Benedict XVI called "my great master."

The first of these men was named Augustine, who lived during the waning days of the Roman Empire and was one of the most remarkable men North Africa ever produced. He studied rhetoric at the famed University of Carthage in order to become a lawyer, but later gave up this plan in favor of a career in teaching. His study of rhetorical philosophy—with an emphasis on pagan Greek thought—resulted in a complete renunciation of Christianity.

He lived, then, an admittedly debauched life—which included keeping a mistress for fifteen years by whom he had a son. In pursuit of opportunities to improve his academic standing, he took teaching posts, first in Rome and later in Milan. It was in Milan that he fell under the unexpected influence of the eloquent Bishop Ambrose. After a long and tortured battle of the soul—described in his classic autobiography *Confessions*—Augustine was converted and baptized under Ambrose's ministry.

Soon the steadfastness, holiness, and genius of Augustine were recognized and he was ordained—though very much against his own objections. And a few years later he was elevated to the bishopric of the city. He was a devoted pastor, but his writing was the means of his greatest impact. During his career he wrote more than a thousand works, including 242 books. Most of these have endured, but he is probably best known for his manifesto of faith, *The City of God*.

According to Martin Luther, this one book "set the very course of Western Civilization." According to John Knox, it is the very essence of "incisive Christian thought applied to the circumstances of this poor fallen world." Thinkers as diverse as Anselm, Petrarch, Pascal, and Kierkegaard all counted *The City of God* as their first and primary intellectual influence. Indeed, this one book has had an astonishing influence on the shaping of Western culture for centuries.

The other man in this tale was named Thomas Aquinas. He was born into an aristocratic Italian family during the high medieval period. Landulph, his father, was Count of Aquino; Theodora, his mother, Countess of Teano. He showed early promise as a student and was marked by a deep and profound piety. When he attended a university and quickly surpassed his professors, his parents hoped he might establish himself as a lawyer or diplomat. Thomas chose instead a life in the Dominican order. The whole city of Naples was said to have wondered why such a noble young man should don the garb of a poor friar.

His family was so appalled that they had him confined for two years in the fortress of San Giovanni at Rocca Secca in hopes that he would come to his senses. He refused to relent, however, and was finally released to a Dominican monastery.

In Paris and Cologne he studied under the most brilliant mind of the age, Albertus Magnus. But it wasn't long before the wisdom of Aquinas outstripped even that of his mentor. After obtaining his doctorate, Aquinas began to write, and his remarkable mind soon made its mark on the world. He was nearly as prolific as Augustine, composing hundreds of works and dozens of books. Yet, like Augustine, his reputation rests on his magnum opus, a systematic theology entitled the *Summa Theologica.*

Like *The City of God,* the *Summa* quickly altered the course of men and nations. Virtually every Roman Catholic theologian since Aquinas has found in the *Summa* all the language, categories, and philosophical frameworks for faith. G. K. Chesterton called it the "North Star of Western thought." Hilaire Belloc called it the "lodestone of orthodoxy." And Pope John Paul II asserted that it was an "indispensable guide to the Christian world and life view."

Given all this, it is tempting to believe that Augustine and Aquinas were very similar men, thinking very similar thoughts. But nothing could be further from the truth. While Augustine categorically rejected the principles of Greek philosophy—including the ideas of Plato and Aristotle—Aquinas embraced them and wove them into his Christian understanding of the world.

Augustine tended to think in black-and-white; Aquinas frequently thought in various shades of gray. Augustine drew a line through all of history—on one side was the City of God, on the other was the City of Man. Nearly every fact, every event, every idea, and every movement could be seen to fall on either side of the divide. Aquinas drew lines of distinction as well, but they were far more complex, subtle, and broad. Augustine thought in exclusively biblical categories, while Aquinas thought in inclusive philosophical categories. Augustine drew inferences from Scriptural ideas; Aquinas drew inferences from Socrates, Plato, and Aristotle. Philosophers and theologians have said that Augustine's ideas were based largely on antithesis, while the ideas of Aquinas were based largely on synthesis. And never the twain shall meet.

So who was Joseph Ratzinger's "great master"? Not too surprisingly, it was Augustine, whose writings were for Ratzinger "a spiritual experience that left an essential mark." Of Aquinas, though, he wrote, "I had difficulties in penetrating the thought of Thomas Aquinas, whose crystal-clear logic seemed to me to be too closed in on itself, too impersonal and ready-made." Though Ratzinger admitted that his trouble in embracing Aquinas may have been caused by the way the author of the *Summa* was presented by his teachers, still the "rigid, neo-scholastic Thomism . . . was simply too far afield from my own questions."

Thus it was that Augustine, the man who defended his faith from encroaching paganism and envisioned a flowering of Christian culture, became the theological mentor of Joseph Ratzinger—the man who would preserve Catholic doctrine for nearly a quarter of a century and then become Pope Benedict XVI.

The postwar years of Joseph Ratzinger's life opened with a heartrending scene. It was in the fall of 1945 when he was just eighteen years old. He had only months before been released from an American prisoner of war camp and had then returned to St. Michael's Seminary with his brother, Georg, to work with the other students in rebuilding the school. After six years as a military hospital, the campus needed work. In time, though, things began to return to something approximating normal. Books were borrowed and courses were held in makeshift classrooms.

Yet it is what happened just before Christmas of 1945 that is so touching. Joseph and his brother decided to organize a reunion of their old classmates from before the war. It was a sweet occasion, but during this time of remembrance they sadly realized how many of their boyhood friends had been killed. "Many had fallen in the war," he later wrote, "and we who had returned home were all the more grateful for the gift of life and for the hope that again rose high above all destruction."

The academic destination of students at St. Michael's was normally the major seminary at Freising. It, too, had been used as a military hospital during the war and classes there were also slow in resuming. Once they did, though,

Joseph found himself attending a seminary filled with eager students. The circumstances at Freising reflected the agonies of the German people in the postwar years. Food was scarce, facilities were cramped, and eighteen-year-olds like Joseph were thrown in with hardened combat veterans in their forties.

There is a telling phrase in *Milestones*, Ratzinger's autobiography, about how these older students viewed their teenage classmates. "It was understandable that many of the older combatants looked down on us youngsters as immature children who lacked the sufferings necessary for the priestly ministry," he wrote later. His explanation of this condescension by the older students, though, is deeply instructive. They held the younger students in low regard "since we had not gone through those dark nights that alone can give full shape to the radical assent a priest must give." It is worth noting that young Joseph absorbed the lesson that suffering is essential to what enables a priest to give himself fully to God. This understanding of hardship as redemptive, as a tool to pry the Christian heart from its selfish moorings, and a means of sharing in the sufferings of Christ remained a central theme in Ratzinger's thinking all his days.

Another image that seems to have impressed itself permanently into his soul was that of the Church as holy refuge from the evils of the world, most recently the evils of Nazism. For Joseph Ratzinger, the Catholic Church was "the locus of all our hopes. Despite many human failings, the Church was the alternative to the destructive ideology of the brown rulers [Hitler's Brownshirts]; in the inferno that had swallowed up the powerful, she had stood firm with a force coming to her from eternity. It had been demonstrated: The gates of hell will not overpower her. From our own experience, we now knew what was meant by 'the gates of hell,' and we could also see with our own eyes that the house built on rock had stood firm."

While there is no question that a young seminarian was justified in believing his Church a refuge from the horrors he had passed, it is also true that not everyone has viewed the Catholic Church during the war years in such heroic terms. Many have spoken of the Catholic Church as riddled with compromise during World War II. Pope Pius XII, the Roman pontiff at the time, has been called "Hitler's Pope," and Catholics have been accused of everything from cheering on the persecution of the Jews to encouraging Hitler's anti-Semitism from their pulpits.

The truth is, as usual, far more complicated. To gain an understanding of Catholic culture in Germany at the time, it might be helpful to look a bit more closely at the life of Michael Cardinal von Faulhaber. It was this man who had driven his shiny black car into a Bavarian village square and so impressed the five-year-old Joseph Ratzinger. It was also this man who sponsored the seminary Joseph attended, who would one day ordain both Joseph and his brother, Georg, as priests, and who has been called Joseph's most important early mentor. Surely his involvement with the Nazis would not only be instructive as a representation of the times but also for the influence he must have exerted on Ratzinger.

Cardinal Faulhaber was ordained in 1892, became a bishop in 1911, and then a cardinal in 1922. His bishopric was in Munich, which put him in regular contact with the Nazi government once it came to power. There is no question that Faulhaber supported the Nazi regime in its early years, at a time when Hitler was paying public lip service to Christianity and some of his policies seemed to be restoring both pride and order to the German people in the wake of World War I. In a 1937 sermon, the cardinal celebrated the support of the Catholic Church for

Hitler's government as "a deed of immeasurable significance for the reputation of the new government abroad." Faulhaber saw Nazism as a protective hedge against atheistic Communism and thought nothing of ordering his nuncio in Germany to produce a birthday celebration for Hitler.

Yet the pro-Nazi stance of his early years must be balanced against his words and deeds once Hitler began showing his true atheistic and anti-Semitic colors. In a sermon as early as 1933, Cardinal Faulhaber preached against Nazi anti-Semitic propaganda in the very year that National Socialism came to power.[1] In 1938, Faulhaber refused to give his approval for a pro-Hitler professor to teach on the theological faculty of the University of Munich. Hitler closed the school in response but the cardinal was unmoved. And during the war, he not only spoke out openly against Hitler's euthanasia program but allowed aid to be smuggled to priests imprisoned in Dachau concentration camp, an act of civil disobedience that would have meant death for all involved had the Nazis learned of it.

What is difficult to understand for many today is the change in perspective of men like Cardinal Faulhaber and of other Germans like him. They welcomed the Nazi party when it first arose because it seemed to be an answer to their nation's woes and a barrier to what they viewed as "godless" Communism. When they saw what Hitler became—a champion of atheism, anti-Semitism, and bloodshed—many courageously took a stand. The judgments of history have lain harshly upon them for their earlier views, but perhaps with time—and a wider knowledge of stories like that of Joseph Ratzinger—these harsh judgments will soften.

What is certain is that Cardinal Faulhaber was a man of sufficient character to inspire at least one idealistic seminarian. As Ratzinger later wrote, "The grand and venerable figure of Cardinal Faulhaber impressed me deeply. You could practically touch the burden of sufferings he had had to bear during the Nazi period, which now enveloped him with an aura of dignity. In him we were not just looking for 'an accessible bishop'; rather, what moved me deeply about him was the awe-inspiring grandeur of his mission, with which he had become fully identified."

While Joseph was growing in his love of his church, he was also broadening his intellectual horizons. He read theology, of course, and was particularly smitten with Augustine. But he was determined not to be confined to theology alone. He wanted to "listen to the voice of man today." He began to devour novels like those of Gertrud von Le Fort, Elisabeth Langgässer, and Ernst Wiechert. He consumed Dostoevsky and then went on to Claudel, Bernanos, and Mauriac. He began to read in the sciences and concluded that the writings of Einstein, Planck, and Heisenberg proved that the mechanistic worldview that had dominated the Western world was yielding to one more open to God.

The truth is that he was undergoing an awakening. Perhaps it was a healing of his heart from the trauma of war or perhaps he was simply allowing himself to feel the burdens and joys of the wider world in a way he never had before. Whatever the case, he was becoming more focused on the human, the personal; the moving dramas of life. Part of this was due to the influence of the rector at the seminary church, a man named Michael Höck. The seminarians called him "the Father" for his kindly and affectionate ways but they were also in awe of him because he had spent five years in the concentration camp at Dachau. What he knew of God he had learned through the most horrible of circumstances, and the men of the school felt the depth and gravity of his inner life. His joy was infectious, as were his prayer life and his passion for loving people.

The example of Father Höck produced a strong sense of community at the seminary. Joseph formed relationships that would last him all his life and he never forgot the music that constantly filled the house in which he lived or the theatrical performances that the school sponsored on festive occasions. Always, though, it was the worship and the liturgy of the Church that were the anchor to his soul. As he wrote of these years in later life, "My most precious memories remain the great liturgical celebrations in the cathedral and the hours of silent prayer in the house chapel."

In 1947, Joseph's two-year course of study at Freising came to an end and he decided to ask his bishop if he could continue his studies under the tutelage of the theological faculty at the University of Munich. The bishop agreed, and Joseph then entered a school which, while still recovering from the ravages of war, would become a gathering place of some of the finest theological minds that Germany had to offer. Men like Friedrich Stummer and Wilhelm Maier in Old and New Testament, Franz Xaver Seppelt in Church history, Richard Egenter and Gottlieb

Söhngen in theology, Michael Schmaus in dogmatics, Josef Pascher in pastoral theology, and Klaus Mörsdorf in canon law would become the stars in Ratzinger's intellectual universe.

He was stepping into the serious study of the Bible and theology when those fields were undergoing great change, when roiling conflicts were promising to redefine religious thinking. For most of the previous century, biblical and theological studies had been dominated by a rationalistic, skeptical approach that attempted to apply the methods of literary criticism to the study of the Bible. The Scriptures came to be understood as the product of human invention, of men writing at a given time in history with a limited worldview and with pronounced cultural biases. Scholars of this school strove to understand the Bible in the same way literary critics might examine Shakespeare or the writings of any human author. This was, of course, deeply offensive to those who regarded the Bible as inspired by God and therefore sacred. The champions of this new approach, though, saw themselves as the vanguard of scientific inquiry into religious matters and maintained that a brave new world of religious truth was about to dawn.

What these scholars concluded—after they had applied the techniques of literary criticism to the Bible—was that much of what orthodox Christians had believed through the centuries was without basis. Jesus was, perhaps, a good man who died for a good cause but he was not God. Men should seek to become like him morally and ethically but should not think he was the author of salvation. What had long been assumed to be the works of Moses or Isaiah were now understood as the compiled works of many men writing sometimes over centuries. All that the Christian faith really had to offer modern man was a system of ethics, largely distilled from the teachings of Jesus. Armed with these ethical convictions, liberal theologians believed that man could fashion a new society, free of religious myth but guided by religious ethics.

The meat grinder of World War I obliterated such idealistic dreams. On the other side of the cataclysm, men could no longer believe in the moral perfectibility of man. Instead, some the most influential scholars of the postwar era began to frame theology from the standpoint of the individual. Once all the myths were stripped away, what might Jesus still mean to an individual in the modern world? Even if modern scholarship questioned who the

Jesus of the first century really was or even whether he really existed, might there still be a subjective experience of Jesus—a Jesus of faith rather than of history—that crept through the pages of Scripture?

These were the questions that theological faculties were wrestling with just at the time that Joseph Ratzinger entered the University of Munich. Men like Rudolph Bultmann and Martin Heidegger were hotly debated, for they were at the forefront of this existential, subjective approach to theology. They pressed the question of what the Jesus of faith might mean to modern man once all the religious myths of the Bible were stripped away. Answering them in defense of more historic Christianity were men like Karl Barth. At a press conference later in his life, Barth would be asked what he knew for certain about religious truth. His answer would send biblical scholars of the old school into apoplexy. He replied simply, "Jesus loves me, this I know, for the Bible tells me so."

Joseph Ratzinger found himself standing between the traditional Catholic approach to Scripture and the insights of the new scholarship. He wanted to be a man of God who lived in conformity to the life of Jesus Christ. Yet he also wanted to be a scholar who brought the best of intellectual tools to the study of the Bible and Church history. He would live in the crucible of the tension between these two approaches to faith all the days of his life.

Given that he would eventually be the head of the Congregation for the Doctrine of the Faith, the branch of Catholicism responsible for doctrinal orthodoxy, it is interesting that one of Ratzinger's favorite teachers at the University of Munich was Wilhelm Maier. A professor of New Testament studies, Maier had been one of the leading proponents of what was called the two-source theory of the first three Gospels. Essentially, he believed that the Gospel of Mark and other sources were the basis of the Gospels of Matthew and Luke. Catholic tradition, though, held that Matthew was the earlier Gospel and was, therefore, the primary source.

Maier's ideas were deemed to be outside the pale of Catholic orthodoxy and he received a decree of *Recedat a cathedra,* which meant "Let him leave his chair," the quaint words the Vatican used to fire a professor of theology. Though Maier went on to be a chaplain in the First World War and then a prison chaplain, the sting of his rejection by Rome never left him. By the time he joined the faculty at Munich and became Ratzinger's favorite professor, he was still brilliant but deeply bitter.

Though his lectures were crammed with eager students in Ratzinger's day, Maier's anger over his treatment was still evident. "He never quite got over the trauma of having been dismissed," Ratzinger later wrote. "He harbored a certain bitterness against Rome, and this extended also to the archbishop of Munich, who, in Maier's view, behaved none too collegially toward him. These reservations aside, Maier was a man of deep faith and a priest who took great pains in the priestly formation of the young men entrusted to him."

Given who he would become, Ratzinger's words are of great importance, for they portray a largeheartedness that he is often accused of lacking. His favorite professor in seminary was a man marked by Rome as a teacher of questionable doctrine. Yet, Ratzinger loved him, had compassion for the pains he had passed, and even saw him as a man of deep faith and a gifted mentor to priests. All of this despite the fact that Maier's soul was marked by bitterness against those who ousted him from his earlier professorship. That in later life Ratzinger will be accused of treating many as Maier was treated makes his early love for this man a telling statement of either a later change in his nature or of an element of his personality that is often ignored.

Ratzinger's own view of orthodoxy is probably best summarized by another episode that occurred during his time at Munich. There had been much debate among Catholic faculties about the matter of the bodily Assumption of Mary into heaven. The Vatican would establish this as Church dogma later but before a final decision was made, many of the best minds were consulted and this prompted widespread debate.

One of Ratzinger's favorite professors, Gottlieb Söhngen, rejected the idea that Mary was taken bodily into heaven at the end of her earthly life and he said so in numerous scholarly gatherings. A Lutheran friend of Söhngen's asked him during the heated debates, "But what will you do if the dogma is nevertheless defined? Won't you then have to turn your back on the Catholic Church?" Söhngen thought for a moment and then answered in words that continued to resonate in Ratzinger's mind for the rest of his life. "If the dogma comes," said Söhngen, "then I will remember that the Church is wiser than I and that I must trust her more than my own erudition." As Ratzinger summarized the episode in his autobiography, "I think that this small scene says everything about the spirit in which theology was done here—both critically and with faith." Clearly, Ratzinger had concluded that the wisdom of the Church was to be trusted in the face of all new ideas.

As he neared the end of his studies at the University of Munich, Ratzinger was invited to participate in a competition in which certain promising theological candidates were encouraged to complete a written assignment. The candidate whose assignment was chosen would not only graduate summa cum laude but would also have the opportunity to proceed straight into a program of study leading to the doctorate. The topic of the written assignment was "The People and the House of God in Augustine's Doctrine of the Church." Ratzinger was thrilled when he heard of it, since Augustine was a favorite topic and since he knew what an honor it was to be invited to compete.

He threw himself into the task and quickly found himself overwhelmed: not so much by the academic work as by the fact that his writing overlapped his preparation for ordination. Having completed his studies at the University of Munich, he was now again under the tutelage of the seminary at Freising as he took courses in the practical aspects of ministry: preaching, catechesis, counseling, and pastoral theology. Fortunately, Georg, who had continued his studies at Freising, was willing to care for all of Joseph's practical needs so that his younger brother could focus on his writing and still prepare for ordination. Also pitching in was Mary, Joseph and Georg's sister, who was working as a legal secretary nearby and who volunteered to type a clean copy of Joseph's work.

Ratzinger turned in his work on Augustine just in time to complete his preparations for ordination. Before long, he would learn that his paper had been chosen and that he would be allowed to pursue the doctorate at the University of Munich. It was a humbling honor and one of the early signs that Joseph Ratzinger was to become one of the brilliant theological minds of his generation. What concentrated his mind now, though, was his looming ordination. It was to be one of the high points of his life. On June 29, 1951, Joseph was ordained by Cardinal Faulhaber in the Freising Cathedral along with forty other candidates—his brother, Georg, among them. It was the Feast of Saints Peter and Paul, and Joseph remembers responding to the liturgical call to the priesthood with the traditional Latin response, *"Adsum,"* "Here I am."

Something else happened as Ratzinger was being ordained that he never forgot and that betrays his attitude toward supernatural signs. "We must not be superstitious," he warns, "but, at the moment when the elderly archbishop laid his hands on me, a little bird—perhaps a lark—flew up from the high altar in the cathedral and trilled a little joyful song. And I could not but see in this a reassurance from on high, as if I heard the words 'This is good, you are on the right way.'" It is not hard to see an older Joseph Ratzinger, writing in 1977, trying to remain always the scholar but finding tender encouragement from the song of a lark at his ordination, much as he had from his baptism with Easter holy water on the day he was born.

By August 1 of the same year, Ratzinger had been assigned as an assistant pastor in the Parish of the Precious Blood in Munich. It seemed the perfect introduction to ministry, for the parish was filled with intellectuals, artists, and high government officials as well as with butlers, maids, and shopkeepers. He would learn what it meant to apply the truth of God to every variety of human life. He was young, he was eager, and he was idealistic.

And he was almost crushed by the load. He had not understood how busy the life of a parish priest could be. He lived in a rectory that was too small and far too hectic for his introverted ways. He had to give sixteen hours of religious instruction at five different levels each week. He heard confessions an hour a day—except on Saturdays, when he heard confessions for four hours straight! On Sundays, he celebrated at least two Masses and gave two different sermons. He was also responsible for the entire youth ministry, buried at least one parishioner a week, and often had baptisms and weddings to conduct besides.

Fortunately, his model at the time was the pastor of the Precious Blood congregation, Father Blumschein, who insisted that priests ought to "glow." This priest gave himself to his people. "To his last breath," Ratzinger exulted, "he desired with every fiber of his being to offer priestly service. He died, in fact, bringing the sacraments to a dying person. His kindness and inner fervor for his priestly mission were what gave a special character to this rectory. What at first glance could appear to be hectic activity was in reality the expression of a continually lived readiness to serve."

Ratzinger thus gave himself to pastoral ministry, attempting to live up to the example of Father Blumschein, all while completing his doctorate in theology. It was a brutal course. Before he could complete his doctorate he had to demonstrate expertise in eight major subjects through both oral and written examinations. Then he had to prepare for an open debate in which he would have to defend theses from all theological disciplines. As difficult as it was, he excelled in every task and began to demonstrate to his mentors that he was an exceptional mind in a soul tempered by war, piety, and pastors of unusual character. In July 1953, he proudly received his doctorate with his mother and father looking on.

Ratzinger now launched into an academic career that can only be described as meteoric. He lectured at the University of Munich until invited to lecture as a full professor at the University of Bonn in 1959. He remained there until 1966, when he took a second chair in dogmatic theology at the University of Tübingen. Troubled by events at Tübingen, as we have seen, he then returned to Bavaria to take a position at the University of Regensburg in 1969. He progressed rapidly there, becoming first dean, then vice president, and later theological adviser to the German bishops. Within a decade, he was named Archbishop of Munich and Freising and ordained on May 28, 1977. One month afterward, on June 27, he was elevated to cardinal by Pope Paul VI.

It was an astonishing rise, but it did not come without difficulty. His path was marked by a series of battles that marked him both as a man and as a thinker. The first of these was the challenge to a book-length paper he wrote to qualify as a professor at the University of Munich. Called a *Habilitation*, it was meant to be the impressive announcement of a great mind on the academic scene. Ratzinger's work initially fell far short of this goal.

He had chosen to write about the idea of revelation in the thinking of St. Bonaventure. He seemed to be making the case that revelation is not the Bible itself, but the act of God in revealing himself through the Bible. Ratzinger rejected the idea that Scripture ought to be called revelation. Instead, like Bonaventure, he maintained that revelation is "something greater than what is merely written down." It is given by the Spirit and since the Spirit has been giving revelation for centuries, an understanding of the truth of the Bible requires tradition as well as the immediate work of the Spirit.

To his academic lords, though, this thesis sounded too modern, too much like the existentialism of Bultmann and Heidegger. It did not help that one of the members of his *Habilitation* committee considered himself an expert in the field and was offended not only that he wasn't consulted but that an upstart should suggest such a novel approach. No, this work would have to be rejected, the committee intimated. It would take years to make the necessary repairs.

Fortunately for Ratzinger, the committee later softened its response. Rather than reject the work, which would have been a humiliating blow to a young professor, they decided to return it for further work. Ratzinger changed his direction and the work was accepted the second time it was submitted. On February 21, 1957, his *Habilitation* was accepted and he was named professor of fundamental theology and dogma at the College of Philosophy and Theology at Freising.

Oddly, the dispute over the *Habilitation* marked Ratzinger as a bit of a radical. He began to be viewed as a brilliant young "new school" thinker, who, if given the chance, would bring change to the Church. This endeared him to his students. It might well have been otherwise. His students experienced him as a shy, soft-spoken man who was of a calm and "pacific" disposition. The word most often used of him by his charges was "gentle." He also had a reputation as a "saintly" man, whose life of prayer and worship was remarked upon throughout campuses where he served.

Yet because he was identified as radical, his students were more intrigued by him than they might otherwise have been. He quickly gained a reputation as a professor of strong convictions who was stubbornly committed to the truth. He was, many said, the smartest man they had ever known and this only made his lectures and the possible re-forming impact of his career of greater fascination to the young.

And so he rose. His reputation as a theologian, a lec-turer, and a spiritual mentor grew. Thus, when Pope

John XXIII announced his desire to convene a new Church council, designed to make the Church more relevant to the modern world, Ratzinger was asked by the archbishop of Cologne, Cardinal Frings, to assist him in his work for the council. It meant that he would be a *peritus*, a theological expert, at the most important gathering of his Church's leaders to occur in his generation.

It must have thrilled both him and young thinkers like him, then, when Pope John XXIII opened what came to be known as Vatican II with these words:

> In the daily exercise of our pastoral ministry—and much to our sorrow—we must sometimes listen to those who, consumed with zeal, have scant judgment or balance. To such ones the modern world is nothing but betrayal and ruin. They claim that this age is far worse than previous ages, and they rant on as if they had learned nothing at all from history—and yet, history is the great Teacher of Life. . . . We feel bound to disagree with these prophets of doom who are forever forecasting calamity—as though the world's end were imminent. Today, rather, Providence is guiding us toward a new order of human relationships, which, thanks to

human effort and yet far surpassing human hopes, will bring us to the realization of still higher and undreamed of expectations.

The council would last from 1962 until 1965 and Ratzinger would be present throughout. He, along with another young theological star, Hans Küng, would advise the German bishops and urge the council on in its reforming work as eagerly as they could from the sidelines. At one point in the conference, Cardinal Frings made a widely quoted speech declaring that the work of the Holy Office—the old office of the Inquisition, which is now called the Congregation for the Doctrine of the Faith— was engaged in "methods and behavior" that "do not conform to the modern era and are a source of scandal to the world." Though the words were spoken by Cardinal Frings, they were almost certainly written by Ratzinger, who may have had the treatment of his old mentor, Professor Maier, in mind.

These were heady days for the young professor. The council had begun with what seemed to him a pure purpose: to open the Church to the modern world without compromising its core message. Ratzinger applauded this

dream and hoped to see it fulfilled. When the council concluded, he had dared to expect a new day of freedom and
growth in his Church.

Already during the council, though, he had seen evidence of compromise that concerned him. Some of the decisions of the council were made more in the manner of
a modern parliament than in the manner of godly men,
he believed. There were party factions and backroom deals.
All of this was odious to the high-minded Ratzinger, who
was now in his mid-thirties and growing weary of the egos
and the unending debate without action. He was also wary
of the rising power of scholars. He believed, as an orthodox Catholic, that the pastoral vision of the church should
inform scholarship rather than the other way around.

For believers, it was a remarkable phenomenon that
their bishops seemed to show a different face in Rome
from the one they wore at home. Shepherds who had
been considered strict conservatives suddenly appeared
to be spokesmen for progressivism. But were they doing
this all on their own? The role that theologians had assumed at the Council was creating ever more clearly a
new confidence among scholars, who now understood

themselves to be the truly knowledgeable experts in the faith and therefore no longer subordinate to the shepherds. . . . It was the Creed that provided the standard also for scholarly science. But now in the Catholic Church all of this—at least in the popular consciousness—was up once again for revision, and even the Creed no longer appeared untouchable but seemed rather subject to the control of scholars.

All of this smacked of rebellion to Ratzinger, who concluded that "resentment was growing against Rome and against the Curia, which appeared to be the real enemy of everything that was new and progressive." He feared that a "sovereignty of the people" was emerging, a "Church from below" that would overthrow the apostolic leaders of the faith. Ratzinger had been filled with expectant joy at the beginning of the council years before, but now he "became deeply troubled by the change in ecclesial climate that was becoming ever more evident."

It may well be that Ratzinger drew a conclusion from his Vatican II experience that has informed his leadership ever since. He was in favor of change as the council began and urged it on with all his skill. Yet he never dreamed that the reform of the Church would exceed the boundaries of historical Christianity. He did not want to break with the past but rather apply the wisdom of the past in a new, more contemporary form to the problems of the present. Yet once the Church moved toward change, engines of rebellion rumbled from within and drove reform toward virtual revolution. Ratzinger believed it had all gone too far, that the needed gentle reforms had been hijacked by a harsher agenda.

Sealing this shift in his thinking was his experience at Tübingen. The 1968 Marxist upheaval had changed him. "Something happened," said fellow professor Hans Küng. "He was deeply shocked by the student revolts. He had big clashes with his most intimate students and assistants." A student on campus at the time, Wolfgang Beinert, remembered that the Marxist uprising among the students "had an extraordinarily strong impact" on Ratzinger, who had been "very open, fundamentally ready to let in new things. But suddenly he saw these new ideas were connected to violence and a destruction of the order of what came before. He was simply no longer able to bear it."

It was a final turn in his worldview. "I had the feeling that to be faithful to my faith, I must also be in opposition to the interpretations of the faith that are not interpretations but oppositions." Clearly, the lessons of the Nazi years, of the theological debates during his seminary training, of his disappointments with Vatican II, and of the horrors of Tübingen had pressed him even more deeply into unswerving Roman orthodoxy.

Ratzinger resigned from Tübingen and took a position at the University of Regensburg in order to "develop my theology in a less agitated environment and also because I did not want to be always forced into the contra position." Clearly, he needed a rest.

He also needed his family. By 1969, the year he began teaching at Regensburg, both his mother and his father had died: his father in 1959 and his mother in 1963, just as his disillusionment with Vatican II was growing. Fortunately, his brother, Georg, was the choirmaster at the cathedral and his sister, Mary, also lived nearby. The three were able to encourage one another in their callings and revive some of the family joy they had known in their youths.

These were good years for the youngest Ratzinger. He wrote some of his best works, helped to start a journal called *Communio*—a quarterly review of Catholic theology and culture that is highly esteemed today—and even built a house on a quiet street, complete with a walled garden. It was an oasis from the troubled times, the perfect refuge for an introvert scholar who wished to teach and think and seek his God without intrusion.

Away from the turmoil of political and doctrinal conflict, he reflected on what he believed to be the descent of the Church and the betrayal of the meaning of Vatican II.

> I am convinced that the crisis in the Church that we are experiencing today is to a large extent due to the disintegration of the liturgy, which at times has even come to be [a] . . . matter of indifference whether or not God exists and whether or not he speaks to us and hears us. But when the community of faith, the worldwide unity of the Church and her history, and the mystery of the living Christ are no longer visible in the liturgy, where else, then, is the Church to become visible in her spiritual essence? Then the community is celebrating only itself, an activity that is utterly fruitless. . . . This is why we need a new Liturgical Movement, which will call to life the real heritage of the Second Vatican Council.

The peace and contemplation of these years were broken, though, by the death of the archbishop of Munich, Julius Cardinal Döpfner. Ratzinger was grieved by the announcement of the cardinal's passing, but his grief was soon interrupted when he was handed a letter informing him that Pope Paul VI had appointed him as archbishop of Munich and Freising. He was troubled and tempted to refuse. When he consulted his confessor, the wise older man immediately responded, "You must accept." Still, he was in turmoil, but after much prayer and soul-searching, he finally accepted and on a Pentecost Sunday in the summer of 1977, he was ordained. One month later, he was elevated to cardinal.

Ratzinger chose as the motto of his office "Co-worker of the Truth," a phrase from the Third Letter of John in the New Testament. It was apt in a manner he could not have expected, for in his new duties he would meet another archbishop, this one from Krakow, Poland. His name was Karol Wojtyla and with this man, Ratzinger would indeed become a "Co-worker of the truth."

THREE

Johannis Paulus Magnus: The Legacy of Karol Wojtyla

They were two different men with different personalities and from different backgrounds. Yet for more than twenty-two years they joined together to preserve orthodoxy and extend their understanding of the legacy of Vatican II. The Roman Catholic Church would enter the new millennium defined largely by their vision.

They had first met in the interregnum between the death of Pope Paul VI and the formal opening of the conclave that elected John Paul I. Karol Wojtyla, the archbishop of Kraków, Poland, was thrilled to find a man who understood the Church's situation as he did. Joseph

Ratzinger, the archbishop of Munich and Freising, felt much the same way. In fact, he later reported that a "spontaneous sympathy" sprang up between them.[1]

They shared the view that the Second Vatican Council had been well-intentioned but ultimately flawed. What began as an attempt to make the Church more relevant in the modern world became, for some, an excuse to challenge longstanding doctrine and to question apostolic authority. Wojtyla and Ratzinger weren't having it. Discovering in each other an ideological soul mate, they began to ponder how the initial vision of Vatican II might be reclaimed, how the Church's former glory could be restored through a renewal of her historic beliefs creatively expressed to a rapidly changing world. Ratzinger articulated their dream. It was time for the Church, he said in an interview, to "dare to accept, with joyful heart and without diminution, the foolishness of truth."[2]

Wojtyla agreed and the two continued to deepen their friendship largely through letters that passed between Kraków and Munich. Then, in 1978, Wojtyla became pope, and tried soon after to bring his friend to Rome. Ratzinger refused. He had duties in Munich, and then there was his teaching. Besides, he had other concerns. He had always been outspoken and even more so since the follies of Tübingen in 1968. Would he be permitted to speak his mind? He doubted it. Vatican officialdom would never allow it, despite the best efforts of his friend who was now John Paul II.

So Ratzinger remained in Munich another year. Then, ever persistent, his friend asked again, inviting him to take over as the prefect for the Congregation for the Doctrine of the Faith. Still, the man from Munich was unsure. He refused again and then reconsidered. He decided to lay out his conditions: he would accept only if he could continue to speak freely on matters he felt strongly about. It was exactly what the pope wanted him to do. And Ratzinger went to Rome.

It was the matching of opposites that has so often throughout history proven effective. Wojtyla was an actor, a mystic, and a poet. He had grown up in a suffering family and a Polish nation under siege, surrounded by death and terrorized first by the Nazis and then by the Communists. He became an ideological warrior who never lost the common touch. He traded in the jeweled slippers of previous popes for brown loafers that allowed him to move more easily among the people. He was handsome, athletic, and playful. Given a hockey stick as a welcome gift from an American city, he twirled it like an airplane propeller before a hundred thousand cheering fans. When teenagers in New York chanted his name, he raised his hands above his shoulders, lifting his hands in hip-hop style, and joyfully began singing "Woo-woo" in response.

Such a reaction to a youthful, boisterous crowd would probably never have occurred to the bookish Joseph Ratzinger. He seldom traveled with the pope, largely because he did not like disrupting his routine. He had grown up the youngest child of a family living in a setting that looked like something out of *Heidi* or the *Sound of Music.* Then the Nazis came. While Karol Wojtyla was attending an underground seminary in Nazi-occupied Poland, Ratzinger was a teenaged conscript in Hitler's army who was reading books when he was supposed to be on the lookout for enemy planes. He would become a brilliant university professor known for his quiet, pious manner. He seemed to have passion only for the truth and this is just what the man who became John Paul II loved about him.

This is not to say that Ratzinger had no sense of humor. He did, but it was dry. His best jokes were told in Latin. He would crack himself up over a play on the pronunciation of a word—but the word was in a language that no one listening understood. A notoriously neat man himself, he once played a joke on a colleague by moving some things on the man's desk. Ratzinger had expected a big laugh but his colleague never even noticed. The orderly scholar's prank would have been funny only at the expense of someone who knew the precise location of every item on his own desk. The rest of the world simply didn't get it.

As bland as he could be, Ratzinger was the right man to stand doctrinal guard for John Paul II. The pope would sometimes be overly mystical and Ratzinger would gently rein him in. The pope would set a doctrinal direction and Ratzinger would put it in the learned form he knew so well. The two would meet over dinner most Friday evenings and chart a theological course for the Roman Catholic future. One week the topic might be new directions in the theology of the Virgin Mary. Another week, the radical ideas of an American university professor might be discussed. John Paul learned to trust Ratzinger as he did few other men. Some at the Vatican even began calling the German theologian by a revealing name: "vice-pope."

Yet there were disagreements. Ratzinger alluded to this, ever so slightly, when he told *Time* magazine in 1993, "We do agree completely on all essentials of Church doctrine and order. We arrive at the same conclusions, and our differences of approach, where they do exist, stimulate discussion." This was standard Ratzinger understatement. Still, he always knew he served at the pleasure of his friend, the pope. On more than one occasion, he encouraged a frustrated colleague with the words of his seminary professor: "I will be convinced that the Church is wiser than I." Always, he submitted his life to counsel of the Church: "It was always my idea to be a Catholic, to follow the Catholic faith and not my own opinions."[3]

So it was that Ratzinger and Wojtyla—the German and the Pole, the Hitler Youth and the Nazi resister, the mystic and the scholar—fashioned their Church for a new generation.

In the first days of his papacy, Benedict XVI spoke openly of the comforting presence of John Paul II, who had died just two weeks before: "I seem to feel his strong hand holding mine. I feel I can see his smiling eyes and hear his words, at this moment particularly directed at me: 'Be not afraid.' " It was heartening for the faithful to hear that the new pope felt inspired by the memory of the old.

Still, the reference prompted many to wonder what else Benedict XVI might be feeling about John Paul II's long shadow as he settled himself upon the throne of St. Peter. Every pope must contend with his predecessor's legacy. Every pope has to redefine the role for himself. Yet John Paul II left a legacy that is unequaled in recent Church history. His more than twenty-five years in the office, his near mythic early life, and his astonishing personal popularity the world over guaranteed him not only a prominent place in papal history but an impact on his own times that promises to be felt for generations. To understand the challenge that now confronts Benedict XVI in the early twenty-first century and to grasp the meaning of his decades at John Paul's side, it is essential to understand the life of the Polish factory worker who became the world's most beloved leader.

Long before Karol Wojtyla became Pope John Paul II, the papacy was already undergoing a historic shift. As recently as the reign of Pope Pius XII, from 1939 until 1958, the regal formality of past centuries was retained. Pope Pius still wore the bejeweled tiara with its three crowns. He was still carried from place to place on a *sedia*, a throne borne aloft on the shoulders of servants. Onlookers were still expected to kneel in his presence.

The beginnings of change came with Pope John XXIII, who followed Pius XII and who was often called "the good pope." Born Angelo Roncalli in the Lombardy village of Sotto il Monte, by the time he came to the papacy he was a heavyset, heavy-smoking diplomat with a classic Roman nose and eyes that were often described as compassionate pools. He had clearly been elected by a conclave that largely expected he would be harmless, that his would be a short-lived, transitional papacy. How he surprised them.

At his coronation he proclaimed, "The secret of everything is to let yourself be carried by the Lord and to carry the Lord." This meant to him that Christ must increase but that the papacy must decrease. He began immediately eschewing the royal trappings of his new role: refusing to be carried in the *sedia*, avoiding the crowns, simplifying the rituals.

He was also a playful nonconformist. Tales of his earthiness spread beyond the Vatican and made him a favorite of the common folk. While he was still cardinal, he was approached by a woman who wore a large crucifix that dangled between two mountainous breasts. *"Quelle Golgotha!"* he proclaimed: "What a Calvary!" On another occasion, he was at work at his desk when a carpenter laboring nearby hit his thumb and began cursing violently. After a moment, the cardinal rose, found the carpenter and demanded, "So, what's this? Can't you say 'shit' like everybody else?"[4]

It was this occasionally bawdy populist who convened the Second Vatican Council. As the grand gathering opened, this man—the "good pope"—arose and courageously rebuked the clerics who saw it as their task to merely scold the modern world. Throughout Vatican II and his papacy, he called the Church to a journey of change. Even upon his deathbed, he uttered the words that became a creed for popes who followed him: "The secret of my ministry is in the crucifix . . . Those open arms have been the program of my pontificate: they mean that Christ died for all, for all. No one is excluded from his love, from his forgiveness."

Paul VI, who succeeded John XXIII in 1963, was less the voluptuary and less the nonconformist but nevertheless followed in his reforming path. He sold the triple tiara popes had worn for centuries and gave the money to the poor. He also made statements that horrified the old Vatican guard but defined the path to a new day for the Church. In his famed document *On Papal Infallibility,* issued in 1967, he stated, "The pope is the most serious obstacle on the ecumenical road." He meant it, and later took the historic steps of meeting with Orthodox patriarch Athenagoras and then giving his own episcopal ring to Michael Ramsey, the Archbishop of Canterbury, as a sign of unity.

The pope who followed Paul VI lasted only a month. He was known as "the smiling pope" and was so unregal in appearance that a commentator, upon hearing news of his election, said, "They've elected Peter Sellers pope."[5] He chose the name John Paul I since he hoped to continue the legacy of the John and the Paul who immediately preceded him. He walked in the path of both men by refusing a coronation and announcing his intention to straighten out Vatican finances and deal with errant clerics. He died of a heart attack while reading in bed before he could even begin.

When the cardinals met a second time in almost as

many months to choose the new pope, they realized they needed something new. They needed youth, vigor, someone who would appeal to the modern world but who also could contend with Communism in a world that remained locked in cold war. They chose the handsome, athletic philosophy professor from Poland, Karol Wojtyla. He would be the youngest pope in 125 years, the first non-Italian in 455 years, and the first pope ever from Poland.

He may have been known to the cardinals of the conclave but the outer world barely knew who he was. When his name was announced from the balcony of St. Peter's on the day of his election, the crowd strained to understand. Someone in the crowd joyfully shouted, "They've chosen a Negro," thinking that the complicated syllables of Wojtyla's Polish name sounded more native to Nairobi than to Kraków.

As the world would quickly learn, he was born on May 18, 1920, in Wadowice, Poland, in a house so close to the cathedral that the priests there knew when Mrs. Wojtyla was baking bread. His father, also named Karol, was a Polish army officer and his mother, Emilia, was a dark-eyed, deeply religious woman who had known much suffering before she married. During her childhood she watched four of her brothers and sisters grow sick, languish, and die. She then lost her mother during adolescence. For comfort she fled to her faith and determined to raise her children in the bosom of the Church.

Her first son was Edmund, a healthy, capable, brilliant child who knew early he wanted to be a doctor. Karol came next. As soon as he was born, his mother began telling neighbors that he would be a great man, a priest. She taught him to cross himself and read Scripture to him daily in hopes of fueling the destiny she dreamed for him. This motherly inspiration, however, would be short-lived. She was often in bed due to inflammation of her heart and kidneys. She became increasingly nervous, weakened, and then withdrew into silence. She died on April 13, 1929, when Karol was eight. Just after her death, Karol's father took him to the Marian shrine at Kalwaria where many of his biographers believe he first acquired his deep devotion to the Virgin, perhaps a transfer of affection from one mother to another.

He was known to his friends as Lolek, an intense, friendly child though one with loner tendencies. He played goalie for the local soccer team and so excelled in school that one of his early teachers said, "He was the nearest to a genius that I ever taught." Always, there was suffering, though. His brother, who had become a successful doctor whom his younger brother revered, died on December 5, 1932, from scarlet fever, which he contracted from one of his patients. Lolek was twelve and his friends remembered that he wept uncontrollably at the funeral, which seemed odd to them because he had never shed a tear when his mother died.

He passed his teen years in the adoring care of his father, a deeply religious man who turned to his God for comfort in his sufferings and for grace to tend his son. Years later, John Paul II would recall of his father, "Day after day I was able to observe the austere way in which he lived. By profession he was a soldier and, after my mother's death, his life became one of constant prayer. Sometimes I would wake up during the night and find my father on his knees, just as I would always see him kneeling in the parish church. We never spoke about a vocation to the priesthood, but his example was in a way my first seminary, a kind of domestic seminary."[6]

In his later teens he began to turn to the theater as an outlet for his gifts and his imagination. He was known among his friends for his bohemian ways, that he grew his hair long and often recited the poetry he memorized by the page. A favorite poem was, prophetically, about a future Slavic pope. Written in 1849 by Juliusz Slowacki, *The Slavic Pope* remained with Karol all his life and took on immense significance once he became the fulfillment of its hopes:

> *This Pope will not—Italian-like—take fright . . .*
> *But brave as God himself, stand and give fight—*

In 1938, Karol moved with his father to Kraków and enrolled in the Jagiellonian University, the school where Nicolaus Copernicus, the astronomer, fashioned his view of the universe and Vladimir Lenin read in the well-stocked library. Karol had developed a deep love of Polish literature and history and hoped to major in these subjects. During the summer of 1939, though, he and his college friends read the news that the Soviet Union had concluded a treaty of friendship with Adolf Hitler. It meant that the Nazis could do what they liked with Poland and on September 1 of that year, the word "blitzkrieg"—"lightning war"—entered the world's vocabulary as a description of the rapid, violent occupation of Karol's homeland.

Before long, Poland's universities were closed and Karol was forced to work as a stonecutter in a quarry by day. By night, he helped to found an underground theater company in order to keep Polish heritage alive. At a time when being discovered would cost him his life, Karol performed patriotic Polish plays in darkened living rooms and gave dramatic recitations of epic Slavic poems.

On February 18, 1941, Karol returned home after a hard day at the quarry to find that the man everyone called "the Lieutenant" had died suddenly and unexpectedly. He blamed himself for not being at his father's side in his final hours. Friends remember that Karol stayed alone by his father's body and prayed for hours without moving, stretched out on the floor in the shape of a cross.

Those hours were a turning point in his life. Not long afterward, he knocked on the door of the archbishop of Kraków's residence and asked if he could become a priest. He knew that the archbishop was running a secret seminary and he knew that by enrolling he was risking his life. Still, he sensed a call, a divine purpose running through his life that reached its fullness at the death of his father.

Aside from this sense of spiritual mission, there may also have been a patriotic motive to his choice. It was widely known that Adolf Hitler had issued an order to one of his commanders in Poland that included these words: "The Poles are born for low labor. . . . There can be no question of improvement for them. The standard of living in Poland must be kept low. The priests will preach what we want them to preach. If any priest acts differently, we will make short work of him. The task of priests is to keep the Poles quiet, stupid, and dull-witted." Hearing of this, Karol Wojtyla may have known exactly what he had to do.

He now passed the Nazi occupation as a student in an underground seminary and an actor in an underground theater. With war's end, much of Poland lay in ruins and Wojtyla was eager to help rebuild both the land and its Christian spirit. He was ordained on November 1, 1946, and said his first Mass the next day on the Feast of All Souls.

His rise in the Church was fueled by his brilliant mind and his courageous opposition to the Communism that ensnared his country. He was sent at the age of twenty-six to study at the Angelicum University in Rome. During his time there he encountered the life of St. John of the Cross and was so moved that he returned to Kraków after graduating and asked to become a Carmelite monk. Wisely, the bishop answered him in words that became a banner over his life: *"Ad maiores res tu es"*—"You are made for greater things."

He treasured these words in his heart, as he did an experience he had in Italy that he didn't mention at first to his superiors in Kraków. While on vacation, he once made his way with a friend to a monastery near Naples where famed mystic Padre Pio often spoke and heard confession. When the little white-bearded monk heard Karol's voice, he dropped to his knees and prophesied that this young Polish priest would one day become pope. This was more than thirty years before the words were fulfilled.

After his years in Rome, he served a number of parishes as priest. He was known as an eager servant and a lover of youth. He often took bands of teens into the mountains to hike, canoe, and camp for days at a time. Part of this was the sheer joy of it and part of it was the fulfillment of his ministry. The Communists did not allow formal youth movements to exist, but Father Wojtyla decided he would start one on his own under the guise of a mere social club.

In 1958, he was named bishop of Kraków. He had been on yet another hike with youth when the news arrived and he left his charges in the mountains to be ordained. Once the liturgy was done, he asked if he could return to his young friends in the woods. The youths were more important to him than his new position.

Perhaps it was good that he felt this way about ecclesiastical status, for his rise in the Church was rapid. After becoming the youngest member of the Polish hierarchy when he was ordained a bishop in 1958, he was then named archbishop in 1964 and made a cardinal by Paul VI in 1967. He was certainly gifted and effective, but at least part of the motive for this speedy ascent was the change in climate happening in Poland. The world was hearing of a "Polish spring," a thawing of relations with the Communist government, and the Vatican wanted both to reward Father Wojtyla's opposition to Communist rule and position him even more strategically to help bring freedom to his land.

It was during these years that he came to know Joseph Ratzinger. The two collaborated without meeting at Vatican II and then met when they were both members of the worldwide Synod of Bishops, an advisory council to the pope. Both were anti-Communist stalwarts—Wojtyla from his life in Poland and Ratzinger from his experience at Tübingen and his knowledge of conditions in Communist East Germany. As they grew better acquainted, they discovered not only their doctrinal unity but also the pleasant blend of their personalities—Wojtyla's engaging personality and philosophical mind, Ratzinger's theological genius and gentle, unassuming ways.

Wojtyla's transformation into John Paul II put the spotlight on the conflict between Christianity and Communism. Now there was a Polish pope, a man known as an ardent anti-Communist who spoke, in a very unpapal manner, about freedom for the peoples of the world. To make his point clear, John Paul returned to his native Poland in 1979—rebuking the "spirit of tyranny," saying Mass before historic crowds on the very grounds the Communist rulers had forbidden to religious activity, and waving his hands with joy as hundreds of thousands chanted, "We want God!"

His visit to Poland spurred the fledgling Solidarity movement, which may have led, two years later, to an assassin's attempt on his life. On May 13, 1981, he was shot during an appearance in St. Peter's Square by a Turk named Mehmet Ali Agca. He almost died of his wounds.

Later, after a near-miraculous recovery, he visited Ali Agca in his prison cell and extended forgiveness. Rather than make the visit a media circus, the pope emerged from his assassin's cell and said, "What we talked about will have to remain a secret between him and me. I spoke to him as a brother whom I have pardoned and who has my complete trust."

This was an unprecedented act by a world leader. Yet there may have been a subtext. Italian intelligence services had learned that Ali Agca was deployed by the Romanian secret police, who in turn were engaged by Russian intelligence to kill the most potent enemy of their regime. Some Vatican experts now believe that the pope knew this when he went into Ali Agca's cell and by extending forgiveness to the man was actually saying to the Russians, "All is forgiven. Let mercy reign." And, in time, the walls came tumbling down.

The trip to Poland, his nobility after the assassination attempt, and, ironically, his unwavering stand against the Western "culture of death" all caused his popularity to soar. With the passing years, he became "John Paul Superstar," as *Time* magazine called him, and that was long before it named him "Man of the Year" in 1994. People grew more focused on the personal life of this pope than they had of any in history. They marveled at his intellect, his humor, at the shelf of books he had written, at the eight languages he spoke, at his moving poetry, and at his amazing vigor. He seemed to be everywhere. Indeed, he was the most traveled world leader in history.

Sometimes it seemed almost absurd. A group of German hikers descending from a high peak in the Dolomites were greeted in their native language by a hiker going the other way. When the group had gone thirty yards farther, one of them turned around and shrieked, *"Gott im Himmel!* It was the pope!"* And so it was. The pontiff had left a group of weary aides three hours behind while he strode on to a distant peak.

He was unique on the world stage because he seemed to straddle what were usually considered unbridgeable liberal and conservative positions. He was staunchly antiabortion, opposed to the ordination of women, and against calling homosexuality anything but a sin. He insisted on biblical morality. Yet, he championed the poor, called the handicapped his "special friends," opposed America's wars in the Middle East, and thought nothing of chastising the president of the United States over the issue of capital punishment. He made statements that caused religious conservatives to squirm: "It can therefore be said that, from the viewpoint of the doctrine of the faith, there are no difficulties in explaining the origin of man, in regard to the body, by means of the theory of evolution."[7] Yet he would turn right around and chastise a South American bishop because he suggested that the Church was too aligned with the rich against the poor. To some, he proffered a confusing mix of ideologies; to others, he delivered a consistently Christian worldview that stood outside the temporal politics of the age.

With the passing of time, though, both his vigor and his shining role on the world stage dimmed. He had broken bones in a fall, undergone a less than successful hip replacement, and then been diagnosed with Parkinson's disease. It was the beginning of a long, slow decline that the Vatican chose not to hide and that was thus on painful display for the watching world.

Yet while his body declined, his mind and spirit became fixed on the end of the millennium. He decided he wanted to prepare his Church for a "fresh work of the Holy Spirit," for a renewal that would coincide with the dawn of a new age. Calling his initiative Jubilee 2000, he began urging his Church to repent in advance of a "new wind of God." He led the way himself. He asked forgiveness of Orthodox believers, Protestants, and Jews for the Catholic sins against them. He became the first pope to apologize for the Church's role in the Holocaust, the first to enter a synagogue, and the first to call the Jews "our elder brothers." He even visited the Wailing Wall in Jerusalem and slipped a prayer of repentance between the surviving stones of the ancient temple.

Clearly, he wanted the Church to get clean in anticipation of a renewing work of God. It broke his heart, then, when the pedophilia scandals became public just as he was hoping for a new holiness in his flock. He endured fiery personal criticism at his handling of the affair and saw the focus of many Catholics diverted from his hopes for a revival of Pentecost in the church of the new millennium. Undaunted, he continued to insist that a great day of Christian unity and revival was just ahead. Indeed, even from his deathbed he issued encouragement to hope and reliance on the Holy Spirit to the crowds in St. Peter's Square.

When John Paul II passed from this world, his last word was "Amen." Many felt that this had been appropriate. His life, to them, was a prayer for peace and renewal. And they hoped that God was listening.

Others were relieved for the "Amen" because they were eager for the "Superstar" papacy to end. They felt, much as John Cornwell expressed in his *The Pontiff in Winter*, that the legacy of the departed pope would be felt "in various forms of oppression and exclusion, trust in papal abso-lutism, and antagonistic divisions. Never have Catholics been so divided . . . Never has the local Church suffered so much at the hands of the Vatican and papal center."[8]

When John Ratzinger was elected pope, he knew that the "shoes of the Fisherman" had become harder to fill during John Paul's reign. He also knew that he was no "su-perstar," no irresistible force of charm and papal energy. Yet he understood that there was something more to John Paul's legacy than the public persona that won global ado-ration. Carefully and for decades, he and his friend had defined a vision of the Church that had to be protected. Who better than him? The one who had met with John Paul II weekly, who extended his doctrinal direction, dis-ciplined those who broke ranks and frequently put the passions of Karol Wojtyla into theological form? It is for these reasons that to understand what kind of pope Benedict XVI might be, we must first understand what kind of guardian of the faith Joseph Ratzinger was as head of his church's doctrinal police.

FOUR

Ratzinger and the CDF: Guarding Holy Tradition

When Joseph Ratzinger became Benedict XVI, both his critics and his admirers began making references to the Inquisition, references that portrayed the extremes of response to the new pope. Those who resented him for his relentless defense of Catholic doctrine called him a modern-day inquisitor and the "heir of Torquemada." He was accused of using "the tactics of the medieval torturer" because he banned university professors who were in favor of abortion or gay rights and he disciplined priests who preached a mixture of Marxism and Christianity. His supporters applauded him for some of

these same acts, one of them saying on network television, "Perhaps we need a kinder, gentler Inquisition to call
the Church into line."

It quickly became obvious that neither Ratzinger's
more strident critics nor his more rabid fans knew much
about the Inquisition. Since the man who is now pope led
the office that was once called the Holy Office of the
Inquisition, perhaps it would be helpful to recall that cruel
season in the history of the Church.

It is a small point but it should be said that the
Inquisition with which Ratzinger is sometimes compared
was not a medieval event. It took place, instead, during the
period of the Renaissance. So, when an overeager young
Ratzinger enthusiast answered a reporter's question about
heretics by saying, "The new pope is going to get medieval
on their ass," he was being as historically inaccurate as he
was being unchristian.

Regardless of when it occurred, though, the Inquisition
certainly represented the Church betraying the message
of its founder. There were witch hunts, torture chambers,
and cruel forced conversions. There were Star Chambers,
mock trials, and brutal repressions. There were burnings,
hangings, dungeon tortures, immolations, mutilations,

and senseless slaughters. There were even fanatical wars, pogroms, and purges.

The name most associated with this nightmare season in history was Tomás de Torquemada, the first Grand Inquisitor of Spain. He was a nephew of the celebrated theologian Cardinal Juan de Torquemada, the confessor to the court of Castile, and the prior of the Dominican monastery of Santa Cruz at Segovia. Known for his incorruptibility and piety, he was chosen by the Vatican to counsel the sovereigns of Castile and Aragon on the problems they faced in their respective Spanish kingdoms.

It seems that the purity of the faith in those lands was thought to be in great danger. Apparently, authorities believed that "false converts" from Islam and Judaism had turned to Christianity purely for material gain. The religious authorities feared that these converts were, in essence, "wolves in sheep's clothing" who would commit outrages and infect the lands of Castile and Aragon with error. Something had to be done, so the reasoning went.

Pope Sixtus IV empowered Queen Isabella of Castile and King Ferdinand of Aragon to establish a formal inquiry into these matters. Torquemada was put in charge of this commission. And that is when the trouble began.

Torquemada began conducting trials—trials that were, by most accounts, mockeries of justice. Indeed, the Grand Inquisitor was so unstinting in his zeal that he actually invented new tortures to secure the confessions he sought.

Accused heretics suffered unspeakable cruelties. They were first required to undergo the auto-da-fé, or the ritual of public penance and humiliation. They would be forced to wear a special sign identifying them as deceivers while they were paraded through the markets and public squares. Then they would be tortured to secure a "valid" confession. There were tools uniquely designed for such moments. Over the years, instruments had been created for probing below the fingernails, stripping the flesh from the spine, pouring molten lead or boiling pitch down the throat, mangling genitalia, breaking bones slowly and systematically with large screws, tearing out the tongue, and dozens of other purposes.[1] Finally, if the accused survived these horrors, they would be turned over to the secular authorities for imprisonment or execution by burning at the stake.

Edgar Allen Poe's short story "The Pit and the Pendulum" captured the terror and inhumanity of such proceedings:

Even while I breathed there came to my nostrils the breath of the vapor of heated iron. A suffocating odor pervaded the prison. A deeper glow settled each moment in the eyes that glared at my agonies. A richer tint of crimson diffused itself over the pictured horrors of blood. There could be no doubt of the design of my tormentors. Oh, most unrelenting! Oh, most demoniac of men! "Death," I said, "any death but that of the pit."

Likewise Dostoyevsky, in *The Brothers Karamazov,* portrays the horror of the Grand Inquisitor, with "his withered face and sunken eyes," actually confronting Jesus just after he had raised a dead child to life again:

The Inquisitor sees everything; he sees them set the coffin down at Jesus' feet, sees the child rise up, and his face darkens. He knits his thick grey brows, and his eyes gleam with a sinister light. He holds out his finger and bids the guards arrest Jesus. And such is his power, so completely are the people cowed into submission and trembling obedience to him, that the crowd immediately makes way for the guards, and in the midst of a deathlike silence they lay hands on Jesus and take him to

the Inquisitor who says: "Tomorrow I shall condemn
thee and burn thee at the stake as the worst of heretics."

Such literary scenes are often matched by historical accounts of the unabashed cruelty of Torquemada and his
followers. *Foxe's Book of Martyrs,* which first appeared in the
late sixteenth century, describes similar horrors under
Bloody Mary—queen of England and the granddaughter
of Ferdinand and Isabella. Likewise, *Howie's Scots Worthies,*
published in 1781, retells the sordid story of similar abuse
in Scotland. Though the number of victims in the relatively brief season of the Inquisition is often highly
inflated—in fact, there were probably less than three
thousand people ever to undergo the ordeal over the
course of a century and a half—it was nevertheless a dark
and oppressive time in the history of the Church.

Clearly, whatever tactics Joseph Ratzinger may have
employed to check what he deemed to be doctrinal error
while head of the Congregation for the Doctrine of the
Faith (CDF), he is not a Torquemada, an inquisitor, or a
torturer in any historic sense. He is, rather, a conservative
Catholic theologian determined to keep his Church in

line, much as he has done for decades at the behest of
John Paul II.

❧

When Joseph Ratzinger became the archbishop of Munich
and Freising in 1977, he was asked what design he wished
for his coat of arms. Already for a thousand years the bishops of Freising had displayed a crest that included the head
of a crowned Moor, a man of that mixed Arab and Berber
race whose armies had troubled Spain for centuries. No
one knew quite why such a figure should grace a Bavarian
bishop's coat of arms, but Ratzinger maintained the em-
blem, as he explained in *Milestones*, as a "sign of the uni-
versality of the Church, which knows no distinction of
races or classes, since all of us 'are one' in Christ."

Yet the new bishop also wanted his crest to say something more. He decided to add to it two symbols drawn
from legends that had special significance to him. The first
was the image of the seashell. He chose it, he said, as a
symbol of "our pilgrimage," of the truth that "We have
here no lasting city." It came from a story associated with

the life of Augustine, who was apparently strolling the seashore one day while contemplating the mystery of the Trinity. Augustine looked up to see a child who was playing with a shell and who kept trying to put the water of the ocean into the shell's little hole. Suddenly, Augustine heard the words, "This hole can no more contain the waters of the ocean than your intellect can comprehend the mystery of God." "Thus for me," explained Ratzinger, "the shell points to my great master, Augustine, to my own theological work, and to the greatness of the mystery that extends farther than all our knowledge."

The second symbol that he added to the coat of arms was from the Bavarian legend of St. Corbinian, the founder and first bishop of Freising. Apparently Corbinian was making his way to Rome when a bear attacked and tore his horse to pieces. The bishop then reprimanded the bear for his crime and, as punishment, required him to carry the horse's load all the way to Rome before he was released from his penance.

This became particularly meaningful to Ratzinger after he read St. Augustine's meditation on Psalm 73:22–23. Modern translations tend to render the words something like, "When my heart was bewildered. . . . I was stupid and ignorant, I was like a dumb beast before you. And yet I am always with you." Augustine understood the word "beast" as a draft animal used for farm work. Hence, this renders the translation as "A draft animal am I before you, for you, and this is precisely how I abide with you." As Ratzinger interpreted this, Augustine "had chosen the life of a scholar, but God had chosen to make him into a 'draft animal'—a good, sturdy ox to pull God's cart in this world . . . Just as the draft animal is closest to the farmer, doing his work for him, so is Augustine closest to God precisely through such humble service—completely within God's hand, completely his instrument."

The symbol of the bear became so meaningful to Ratzinger that he has now made it, along with the seashell, part of his papal crest. Already in 1977, it had become for him a portrayal of his personal mission. As he concluded in the final words of his biography, "I have carried my load to Rome and have now been wandering the streets of the Eternal City for a long time. I do not know when I will be released, but one thing I do know: that the exclamation applies to me too: 'I have become your donkey, and in just this way am I with you.' "

These symbols of the shell and the bear are deeply re-

vealing of Ratzinger's sense of humility and spiritual burden. He is a theologian who often spends his days contemplating the knowledge of God, yet he realizes that
man is too finite ever to grasp this knowledge fully. He will
serve his Lord by mining the truth of God but he accepts
the reality that he will never achieve perfect understanding. He is also a servant, a "draft animal," who carries a
heavy load hoping one day to be released. Until he is, he
understands that he is closest to his Lord when he is carrying the heaviest load, when he is laboring in the presence
of his Master.

While it is possible that these sentiments merely reflect
the style of the Catholic hierarchy—in which a high office
is seen as something to be prayed against and then accepted with expressions of unworthiness—the greater
likelihood is that Ratzinger is speaking from the heart. He
does indeed bear a burden—the burden of being thrust
into the glare of public responsibility. He is, as we have
seen, a man more at home in the scholarly life, at peace
among books and prayer. Those who have tasted that life
can understand why Ratzinger would long, even after
decades, to return to it. Yet he willingly sacrifices this hope
and assumes his burden in the service of his Lord. He will

fulfill his commission, his apostolic ministry, and trust that this will bring him closer to his God.

It is significant that already in 1977, when he was a newly minted archbishop, he was thinking of his ministry as a burden and hoping one day to be released from it. If this is true, John Paul II's invitation in 1981 to head the Congregation for the Doctrine of the Faith (CDF) must have seemed like a summons to further miseries. Perhaps this explains why Ratzinger refused the invitation not once, but twice. He wanted the life of a pious scholar, not a theological warrior. This may also explain why he tried to resign from the CDF, first in 1991 after a decade in office, then again in 1996, and once more in 2001.

Ratzinger knew that ever since Pope Paul III established the Sacred Congregation of the Universal Inquisition in 1542, it had been a locus of controversy. Though its stated assignment was simply to "safeguard the faith, proscribe false doctrines, and defend the Church from heresy," according to the *Encyclopedia of Catholicism*, its history, as we have seen, abounded with doctrinal conflict, persecution, censorship, torture, and execution. It was this office that had famously censured and then condemned Galileo for being right about the nature of the solar system. It was also this office that maintained an *Index of Forbidden Books* until as recently as 1966. Even when Pope Paul VI changed its name in 1965 to the Sacred Congregation for the Doctrine of the Faith, the office was constantly embroiled in theological firestorms. Ratzinger knew all this. Indeed, it was his decision to drop the word "Sacred" from the CDF's name.

The contemporary headquarters of the CDF would probably disappoint those who led the Holy Office of the Inquisition through its more violent days. It stands just to the left of St. Peter's Basilica and behind the Bernini colonnade that encloses the famous square. It is a bland, fortresslike building—complete with thick bars on the windows—called the Palazzo del Sant'Uffizio, inside of which are the offices for the three dozen or so staff members of the CDF and until recently, of course, the office of Joseph Ratzinger.

Ghosts of inquisitors past would probably also be disappointed with Ratzinger himself. He is, unlike many of them, no hardened interrogator. Instead, even his detractors see him as mild mannered and disarming. John Allen, a Ratzinger critic and author of *Cardinal Ratzinger: The*

Vatican's Enforcer of the Faith, has written that the former CDF head is

> by most accounts, a charmer in person. The silver hair
> and dark eyes that look so piercing in photographs have
> a different effect up close; he seems more avuncular, al-
> most frumpy, with a coy smile. Yet he is also reserved,
> often preferring to use the formal German term "Sie"
> rather than the familiar "du" in conversation, even with
> people he's known for decades.

Yet Allen also contends what many in the Roman Catholic Church have come to believe: that Ratzinger's exercise of power at the CDF was "not what Jesus had in mind." Rather than gently correcting error and leading by holy example, Allen says, Ratzinger "drew lines in the sand and wielded the tools of his office on many who crossed those lines." This, in his view, left "the church more bruised, more divided, than at any point since the close of Vatican II."

Allen is not alone. Paul Collins, author of *The Modern Inquisition* and a priest himself until he came into conflict with the CDF in the late 1990s, has not only argued that Ratzinger abused his authority as prefect but believes that the office ought to be abolished. He writes,

> It would be great if we had a church where one could simply dismiss what inquisitors like Ratzinger say and do, but that's not Catholicism today. Too many real people are being hurt by his power plays, and somebody has to speak on their behalf. If our commitment to the marginalized means anything, it has to apply to the marginalized inside the church. That means challenging the likes of Ratzinger when they refuse to ordain women or when they silence theologians or in other ways try to squelch the gospel.

The list of prominent professors and clerics who might echo Collins's sentiments is long indeed. There is, of course, the famed theologian Hans Küng, who, despite being a friend of Ratzinger's since Tübingen and having worked with him at Vatican II, has run afoul of the CDF time and again. There is also Leonardo Boff, who as a leading proponent of liberation theology was a victim of the Vatican's ire on more than one occasion. The list might continue with names like Lavinia Byrne, Jeannine Gramick, Robert Hugent, and Tissa Balasuriya.

Perhaps most famous of all those who ran afoul of John Paul II's—and thus Ratzinger's—doctrinal line was Oscar Romero, the archbishop of San Salvador. Though he died before Ratzinger became prefect of the CDF, he has nevertheless become a symbol of resistance to the Vatican's alleged intolerance in recent decades. Romero tried to alert his Church and the world to the murderous policies of the Salvadoran government in the 1970s. His priests were routinely shot and the children in his churches were often kidnapped. He looked to John Paul II for help. Instead, he was accused by Church leaders of inciting "class struggle and revolution." During a trip to Rome to answer these charges, Romero was rebuffed by the pope and returned home in anguish, only to be assassinated one month later while saying Mass. His personal courage and a popular film on his life, called simply *Romero*, have made him a lasting symbol to many in the face of Rome's sometimes callous ways.

Stories like Romero's are at the heart of the divisions rending the Catholic Church today. On the one side are the progressives, the dissidents, who wish to see a more modern, socially active church. These see Joseph Ratzinger as blocking the way of the Catholic Church that the present age desperately needs. On the other side are the traditionalists who, above all, wish to preserve the great doctrinal heritage of the Church. Ratzinger, their champion, a stalwart of the faith in opposition to the immoral secularism of this age. Though the modern media sometimes view this cleavage in terms of the personalities of John Paul II or Joseph Ratzinger, they are actually rooted in theological differences that are crucial to understanding not only Ratzinger as the head of the CDF and his likely ministry as Benedict XVI, but also the future of the Church.

It is often difficult for Protestants and some non-Christians to understand Catholic controversies over doctrine. For conservative Protestants, questions of doctrine are answered simply by asking "What is biblical?" Ever since Martin Luther's emphasis on *sola Scriptura*—"only by Scripture"—during the Reformation, Protestants have defined their doctrinal positions largely in terms of the Bible alone. The question of what is true is the same as the question of what is biblical. Though some Protestant denominations have moved in a more liberal, modernist direction, even they define themselves in the terms of biblical inter-pretation. An advocate of gay rights in the Episcopal Church, for example, will strive to make his case from the writings of Paul. A proponent of abortion will contend that the Bible is silent on the matter and therefore it is a matter of conscience for each believer, but the touchstone of truth is always the Bible.

For Catholics, it is not the Bible alone but also tradition that must be consulted. Since the Bible as believers know it today did not come into existence until late in the third century, and since it was the Church under the leadership of the Holy Spirit that decided what Scripture was to be—which books of which first-century authors were to be considered authoritative—Catholics believe that the wisdom of the Church as led by the Spirit continues to be a matter of importance. God had spoken through Scripture, yes, but God also continued to speak through the counsel, the tradition, of the Church. In other words, Catholic theology teaches that the Holy Spirit did not "write the Bible and then return to heaven" as one priest put it wryly, but rather that the Holy Spirit continued to speak through the leaders of the Church itself.

The question for Catholics in any generation, then, is

whether those in apostolic authority—those anointed leaders who according to tradition follow in the footsteps of the original apostles—are being led by the Holy Spirit. In ages past, when the idea of living under the authority of human leaders was an accepted part of life, the Holy Spirit's guidance of the Church's leaders was assumed. Today, when democracy reigns and even the Catholic Church, at least in the West, is closer to the "Church from below" or the "Church of the people" that Ratzinger feared in the wake of Vatican II, it is not uncommon for laymen to question the spiritual authority of their Church, at least on certain doctrines.

This explains why a man like Charles Curran, who differed with the Church's position on sexuality as expressed in *Humanae Vitae* in the late 1960s and lost his license to teach theology in Catholic universities, can insist, "The Holy Office cannot have a copyright on what it means to be a Catholic." Curran, like many dissident Catholics, believes that the Holy Spirit is still offering guidance but that the Church, at least on sexual matters, is failing to listen. It would be the same with Catholic advocates of women's ordination, liberation theology, abortion, gay rights, and marriage for priests. The Spirit, they might say, is speaking but the Church leadership, primarily John Paul II and Joseph Ratzinger, is not listening.

By contrast, conservatives accuse dissidents of being influenced by the evils of the world and thus espouse a more democratic Church in order to plant those evils in Christian soil. These more traditionalist Catholics believe that the Holy Spirit has already defined a body of doctrine throughout the centuries of Church history. They maintain that dissident Catholics are merely in rebellion and want the voice of democratic man to prevail rather than the voice of the Holy Spirit. John Paul II spoke to this when he told *Time* magazine's Wilton Wynn, "It is a mistake to apply American democratic procedures to the faith and the truth. You cannot take a vote on the truth. You must not confuse the *sensus fidei* [the 'sense of the faith'] with 'consensus.' "[2]

Joseph Ratzinger puts the matter even more bluntly. Asked in *The Ratzinger Report,* his his book-length interview with Italian journalist Vittorio Messori that became a Catholic bestseller, whether he believed there are still heretics in the world, he said, "Heretics and heresies—characterized by the new Code as 'punishable offenses against religion and the unity of the Church'—exist, and ways have been provided to protect the community from them." It is this very concept—that heretics must be dealt with to protect the true community of faith—that motivated Ratzinger during his years at the helm of the CDF.

For Ratzinger, the tradition of the Church is a sacred trust that must be painstakingly guarded from sin, error, or license. This is because "the Church is His [God's], not ours." So intensely does Ratzinger feel this commission that he is even willing for Christianity to become smaller and less culturally significant if that is the price of purity. In *The Ratzinger Report*, the then-cardinal said,

> Today more than ever the Christian must be aware that he belongs to a minority and that he is in opposition to everything that appears good, obvious, logical to the "spirit of the world," as the New Testament calls it. Among the most urgent tasks facing Christians is that of regaining the capacity of nonconformism, i.e., the capacity to oppose many developments of the surrounding culture.

Ratzinger clearly believes that the Catholic dissidents he has disciplined have been ensnared by the spirit of the age. For the sake of the Church and for their own sake, he has taken action against them. This, he believes, is redemptive, for "excommunication . . . is to be understood as a corrective punishment, that is to say, as a punishment that does not punish him [the heretic] but rather aims much more to correct, to better him."

To those who accuse Ratzinger of pressing his own theological agenda as head of the CDF, eminent American Catholic author Michael Novak responds that they simply do not understand the character of Catholic doctrine. "John Paul II and Joseph Ratzinger were not attempting to control others with their own idea. Instead, they were controlled by something themselves: by the doctrine of the Church. Their only concern in the face of new ideas was 'What has scripture to say about this' and 'What has been the doctrine of the church.'"[3]

Novak even suggests that Ratzinger's pursuit of leading dissident churchmen and professors as head of the CDF may have been calculated for effect. He explained with a story about Calvin Coolidge, who was once asked how the presidency might be improved. "Cool Cal" replied, "It would help if the president could assassinate one person every year." Asked if just one person would be enough, Coolidge replied, "No, but everyone else would worry it was their turn and that would get the job done." Novak's point is that when Ratzinger disciplined leading proponents of dangerous ideas, it may have had the effect of pulling others into line without the CDF having to act against them.

Ratzinger's supporters applaud this vigilance in guarding the truth. Among conservatives—many of whom call themselves "Ratzinger Catholics"—there is a sense of gratitude that someone is standing watch against modernism and heresy in the Church. Rather than yield to philosophical trends and fashions, Ratzinger "thinks in centuries" and understands himself as the doctrinal guardian for the generations that will come after him.

Ratzinger may also have transformed the CDF in ways that his critics failed to understand. Father Augustine Di Noia, theological adviser for the U.S. bishops' conference, contends that Ratzinger made changes at the CDF that liberals ought to respect. "This was one of the most secretive institutions in the church for hundreds of years," he insists. "It cannot be underestimated that he opened it up. Its procedures, its staff, are all now a matter of public record. In the cloud of controversy that surrounds him, that has sometimes been forgotten. He has transformed it into a very modern office."[4]

Part of this new openness arrived, surprisingly, on the wings of Ratzinger's media skills. Father John Rock, who worked for Ratzinger at the CDF from 1990 until 1995, recalled that the prefect had a winning way with the press. In contrast to the unwillingness to engage modern ideas that marked early administrations at the CDF, Ratzinger held press conferences and showed remarkable command of the philosophies then shaping society. "He met often with the Italian press and truly won them over," Father Rock remembered. "They respected him because of his candor, which was not at all typical of a curial bishop."[5]

Conservative Catholics also maintain that critics fail to give Ratzinger credit for welcoming new movements into the Church. For example, he supports the Catholic Charismatic renewal, which is a merging of Catholicism with the Pentecostal emphases of speaking tongues, healing, expressive worship, and miracles typified in American Protestant culture by the likes of Oral Roberts, T. D. Jakes, and Pat Robertson.

This has surprised some, who naturally expected Cardinal Ratzinger the conservative theologian to dismiss the messy Charismatic movement. Instead, he has welcomed it. Noting that Pope John XXIII prayed for "a new Pentecost," he has said in *The Ratzinger Report,*

> His prayer did not go unheard. In the heart of a world
> desiccated by rationalistic skepticism, a new experience
> of the Holy Spirit has come about, amounting to a
> worldwide renewal movement. What the New Testament
> describes . . . as visible signs of the coming of the Spirit is
> no longer merely ancient, past history: this history is becoming a burning reality today.

Though Ratzinger has urged temperance in dealing with the Charismatic movement—"It is essential, above all, to maintain a balance, to beware of an exclusive emphasis on the Spirit"—he also seems to rejoice that the Holy Spirit is working in a manner that supersedes the planning of Church leaders. "I find it marvelous that the Spirit is once more stronger than our programs and brings himself into play in an altogether different way than we had imagined. In this sense the renewal, in a subdued but effective way, is afoot."

American Catholic Charismatic leader Ralph Martin

says that Ratzinger has been a long-time supporter of the renewal and has often addressed Charismatic Catholic conferences. In fact, during his time at the CDF, Ratzinger authored documents that stated the church's position on the Charismatic movement in an encouraging and positive tone. "He is as much in support of the renewal as John Paul II was," Martin says, "perhaps even more so."[6] As confirmation of Ratzinger's support, Martin relates that within days of becoming Benedict XVI, the new pope addressed a conference of Charismatic Catholics at Rimini in Italy. "He is one of us," says another member of the movement, "and this surely shows that he is not only a man of truth but a man of the Spirit, not just a scholar but a follower of Jesus as well."

Though it is unlikely that Ratzinger's critics will be won over by such testimony, it may nevertheless help to answer the charge that he is attempting to place a tight-fitting, antiquated doctrinal straitjacket on the Church. Instead, he sees himself as the caretaker of a sacred tradition. He believes that the fruit of his work is not measured in months but in centuries. His sense of duty may well have been captured by philosopher Jacques Maritain, who wrote, "The important thing is not to be a success. The important thing is to be in history bearing witness." It is this burden—this sense of obligation to historic truth—that he now continues to carry in Rome. He will not, unlike the bear in the legend of St. Corbinian, find release. For he is now Benedict XVI, and he will stay in Rome and carry his burden until the end of his days.

FIVE

Habamus Papam:
"We Have a Pope!"

When Joseph Ratzinger was elected to the papacy and chose the name Benedict XVI, it was widely rumored that he had selected the name because the previous Benedict's reign lasted only seven years. Given that he was a seventy-eight-year-old man, some believed that Ratzinger was signaling the likelihood of his being a short, transitional tenure as head of the world's 1.1 billion Roman Catholics.

Yet to believe such a thing is to misunderstand Joseph Ratzinger. His life has formed him into a man with a mission, a visionary with a strong sense of what his Church ought to be. Perhaps just as important, he is a scholar given to careful reflection, a historian who thinks in layers of time, and a churchman who gravitates to symbols and signs. He did not choose the name Benedict as a promise that he would serve relatively briefly and harmlessly. Rather, he chose the name as a symbolic statement of what he intended to be—and to understand this one must first consider some of the Benedicts who have preceded him.

Of the religious leaders who have borne the name Benedict before Joseph Ratzinger, some were "anti-popes" who were considered "pretenders to the throne" by the Catholic Church and others lived lives that are largely lost to history. The first, and arguably the greatest, was not even a pope. He was born in a small town near Rome in AD 480, in the waning days of the empire. As a teenager he left the environs of Rome for solitude, in the words of his chronicler, "Giving over his books, and forsaking his father's house and wealth, with a mind only to serve God, he sought for some place where he might attain to the desire of his holy purpose; and in this sort he departed from Rome, instructed with learned ignorance and furnished with unlearned wisdom."[1]

He became a hermit and lived in a cave above a narrow,

gloomy valley, penetrating the mountains not far from the old ruins of Nero's infamous villa. He remained there for three years. Though he sought distance from the world, his reputation for wisdom and miracles drew seekers to the valley beneath his cave. In time, a company of young men gathered around him and he began teaching them the life of prayer and separation from society. Eventually, he built some twelve monasteries in the valley and in each of these he placed a superior with twelve monks. He himself lived with a handful of the most promising young men, whom he personally taught. It was in this way, serving as the father or abbot, that he developed and implemented his famous *Rule*.

This *Rule*, or guide to the community of faith, laid the foundations for Western monasticism—and thereby brought about the first great reformation of the Church, provided the spiritual impetus for the spread of Christianity throughout Europe, and helped to transform the raucous Dark Ages following the fall of the Roman Empire. As Joseph Ratzinger once declared in an interview, the monasteries under Benedict's *Rule* "proved to be an ark of survival for Western civilization."

Though this man, now known as St. Benedict of

Nursia, is remembered as a father of monasticism, he is also, perhaps indirectly, a father of the Western intellectual tradition. The monasteries he founded were havens of quiet and prayer, which in time permitted study and scholarship. With the passing centuries, Benedictines who once grew crops and herded cattle began to copy manuscripts, preserve languages, and develop vast theological systems. As the monasteries became teaching centers, they gave birth to the great European universities, an attempt to apply the Benedictine creed—*ora et labora*, "prayer and work"—to the academic life and calling. This scholastic tradition refashioned Europe and gave the world the transforming engine of Western education.

It was because St. Benedict laid the foundation for much of what Europe became that Pope Paul VI named him the "Patron Protector" of Europe in 1964. There can be little doubt that Joseph Ratzinger took Benedict's name as his own, in part, to identify himself with this father of European learning and piety.

Another Benedict whom Ratzinger surely chose as a symbol of his hopes was Benedict II. Little is known of this pope. He was elected in AD 684 and reigned less than a year. Yet, during his few months in office he secured, with a single act, freedom for the European church that allowed it to flourish for centuries.

It happened in this way. By the time Benedict II ruled, the Church in Europe was controlled by the Byzantine state, headquartered in Constantinople. This meant that all major decisions, including clerical appointments, had to be confirmed by governing authorities thousands of miles from the capitals of Europe. Benedict II obtained a decree from the Byzantine emperor that either abolished imperial confirmations altogether or made it possible to secure them from Church authorities in Italy. The result of this seemingly minor act was to free the Christian Church in Europe from Byzantine control—and from the vestiges of the ancient world—so that it could thrive in the centuries that followed.

For this historic act, Benedict II was also later declared to be a patron saint of Europe. Again, Joseph Ratzinger, eager to work for Christian renewal in Europe, certainly drew inspiration from this Benedict's life when he chose his papal name.

Another source of inspiration must have been Benedict XV, who served as pope during the First World War. Though he reigned for only seven years, he is remembered for noble efforts to bring an end to the horrors of global conflict. Realizing that the "war to end all wars" might destroy the grand heritage of Europe, he devoted himself to mediating a peace. He proposed a "Christmas Truce" in 1914 to prevent, as he said, "the suicide of Europe." The combatants refused to hear and concluded secret treaties that bound the allies to ignore papal peace initiatives. Benedict XV was left to content himself with mobilizing his Church to care for the wounded and the dispossessed. Still, he was a good shepherd to his flock, a pontiff who tried to use his power to save his beloved Europe from self-destruction.

It is not hard to imagine that this legacy played in the mind of Joseph Ratzinger as he chose his papal name. In St. Benedict, he had a model of piety and learning who laid the foundation for Christian Europe. In Benedict II, he had the example of a courageous statesman who secured European religious liberty. And in Benedict XV, he had the image of a political prophet who sought to save Europe from the devastation of her soul.

Given his declared intention to call Europe to her former Christian glory, champion religious liberty in the world, and work to bring an end to this generation's wars, it is clear that Joseph Ratzinger hopes, as Benedict XVI, to extend the historic legacy of his chosen name. Indeed, it may be that he intends the name as a means of summoning the spirit of the Benedicts whose vision he now seeks to fulfill.

At 9:37 on the night of April 2, 2005, the sounds of a special Mass arose from St. Peter's Square in Rome into the uppermost rooms of the Vatican's Papal Palace. According to several witnesses, the rhythmic drone of the crowd below—"Lord, hear our prayer"—reached the ears of the dying Pope John Paul II. Turning his head slightly to the window through which the voices came, he hoarsely whispered, "Amen." It was the last word he spoke in this life.

After John Paul's personal physician, Dr. Renato Buzzonetti, confirmed that the pontiff was indeed gone, the ancient traditions began. A thin, white cloth was placed over the pope's face. The *camerlengo,* or chamberlain—whose job it is to preside over the Church between popes—gently called John Paul's given name, Karol, three times. There was, of course, no response. It was ecclesiastically official: the pope was dead. His ring was removed. It would be ceremonially destroyed later and the pieces placed in his coffin. Archbishop Leonardo Sandri then went to the balcony of the basilica and announced to the teeming crowd in St. Peter's Square, "The pope has returned to the house of our Father."

Immediately, members of the international press began wondering if some of the traditional methods of confirming the death of a pope had been used. Had a cardinal held a candle in front of the pope's mouth to see if it would flicker? Had someone tapped his head with a silver hammer? Vatican authorities confirmed that these methods were no longer used. No, it was all much simpler than that. Now, with the announcement of John Paul's death made, the doors of his papal apartments were sealed with ribbons and red wax until a new pope was chosen.

The Vatican, which had long anticipated the passing of this pope, seemed to be well prepared. Immediately it announced the traditional nine days of mourning called the *novemdiales*. The funeral would take place on April 8, officials declared, after a four-day public viewing of the body beneath the dome of St. Peter's. On April 18, the conclave to elect the new pope would begin. As papal spokesman,

Joaquin Navarro-Valls, said at a press conference, "We are prepared. We are good at this kind of thing."

As ready as the Vatican may have been, it could not have prepared for the global outpouring of grief that ensued. During the days leading up to the funeral, an estimated four million people poured into St. Peter's Square, turning the sacred site into a scene that some compared to Woodstock. Mourners wept, sang, and hugged grief-stricken strangers as though they were long-lost friends. Priests heard impromptu confessions and were repeatedly asked for stories of "il Papa." Youths of widely varying na-tionalities gathered in small groups, lit candles, and sang songs or recited the Hail Mary. A reporter interviewed one of these teens and discovered that she was a Protestant. Why did she recite the Hail Mary, then? "I just want to be part of his life," she said, echoing the heartfelt cry of millions.

An article by Kathleen Parker in *USA Today* suggested that this flood of feeling was due to the world's need for a father. Given that an estimated 70 percent of those filling St. Peter's Square were youths, Parker suggested, "If you're the child of a broken family, perhaps one without a father— or an adult awed by rare moral courage— a doc-trinaire, orthodox pope might seem just the ticket.

Perhaps even a godsend." Some commentators agreed. Other insisted that this astonishing wave of emotion was a sign of the new generation's interest in faith. Still more theories were advanced, but it didn't really seem to matter. Whatever the cause, the Vatican seemed at times almost overwhelmed. Sermons and public announcements were often interrupted by crowds chanting *"Santo! Santo!"* a demand for the Polish pope to be made a saint.

When the funeral was finished and the body of John Paul II was interred in the vaulted crypt below St. Peter's— in a tomb once occupied by John XXIII—the world's attention turned to the matter of a new pope. What kind of man would the cardinals choose now? Would they hope for another "Superstar" or would they try to find someone who didn't keep things in such a stir? Would they dare to choose a Third World pope? Perhaps someone less rigid and old school?

Some Vatican watchers expected that the force of John Paul II's popularity would send the cardinals scrambling for an even more nontraditional successor, for a man who might exceed even John Paul II's popular appeal. If this was true, the most likely man was Francis Arinze of Nigeria. His ready smile and gentle wit had already begun to make him a beloved figure in Rome. It was widely known that he had been raised in an African tribal religion until he chose of his own volition, at the age of nine, to become a Roman Catholic. He entered a junior seminary at fifteen and was ordained a priest eleven years later. He proved to be an astonishingly effective leader. During his time as the archbishop of Onitsha—to which he ascended after serving as the world's youngest bishop—the number of Catholics there nearly doubled.

Still, even some who yearned for a Third World pope were concerned that the Church of Rome was unprepared for a man of African descent to occupy St. Peter's throne. Their choice for a non-European figure with pop-culture appeal was Oscar Maradiaga, archbishop of Tegucigalpa, Honduras. Fluent in eight languages and with degrees in philosophy, theology, clinical psychology, and psychotherapy, Maradiaga had been ordained in 1970 and installed as a bishop eight years later. In 1993, John Paul had made him archbishop.

His appeal was partially that he was only sixty-two, ten years younger than Arinze, but also that he was . . . cool. He often spoke of collecting Mickey Mouse and Donald Duck comic books in his youth. He played saxophone, loved jazz, and had a passion for aviation that bordered on addiction: he not only flew his own plane but once built a mock-up of a cockpit in the same house where he kept the more than three hundred model planes he had assembled.

Maradiaga had appeal, as well, because he was a conservative in the manner of John Paul II but with a Third World perspective. He understood that South and Central American liberation theologians had not meant to deny the faith, as some in Rome alleged. They merely wanted justice for the poor. He was also was critical of the United States for exporting liberal views on abortion and contraception to its neighbors. It was an opinion shared by most of the electing cardinals, as was the belief that debt relief for Third World countries was an idea whose time had come.

Many Vatican experts, however, believed that the conclave would never elect a Third World pope. Surely the Italian cardinals would vote as a bloc and prevent it, they observed. If so, the likely choice would be Dionigi Tettamanzi, the archbishop of Milan. Sometimes described as "the Italian John Paul II," Tettamanzi was conservative, moralistic, and charming. He had raged against gambling in Italy—"Man is not made for games; games are made for man"—and had sided with John Paul II on matters of homosexuality, female priests, and contraception.

At seventy-one, Tettamanzi was old enough to insure against another twenty-five-year papacy but still of age to wield a winning style with the public. He was short and round, not unlike John XXIII, and did not take offense when a Scottish cardinal famously suggested in 1999 that he wasn't dignified enough to be pope by saying, "Who's the wee fat guy?" He loved to wade into crowds and play to the press. When he visited the racetrack at Monza, he ended up driving Ivan Capelli's red Mercedes for a few turns. He later said that he often drove his own car much faster on the streets of Milan. The racing-crazed Italians loved it. The Italian press made much of the fact that Tettamanzi was the only papal candidate whose mother might intrude in Vatican affairs if he was elected: she was ninety-four at the time and appeared frequently in photos and interviews.

There were other candidates whom the Italians might approve, though. Angelo Sodano, an Italian and the Vatican's version of a prime minister, was chief among them. Many remembered him as the man who worked the words "John Paul the Great" into a requiem service.

The crowd cheered at the mention of their hero and Sodano's candidacy for pope moved to center stage as a result. There was also Vienna's Cardinal Christoph Schoenborn, who won widespread praise when he cleaned up a sexual abuse scandal that had rocked his diocese, offering heartfelt apologies long before the Vatican even acknowledged there was a problem. Many thought he might be the man to lead a church riddled with scandal.

Noticeably absent from most lists of *"papabili"*— informal Italian for "pope-ables"—was the German cardinal Joseph Ratzinger. Though he was unquestionably the most powerful official in the Roman Catholic Church under John Paul II, pundits could not envision him as pope. Peter Hebblethwaite, in his prophetic booklet, *The Next Pope*, explained why.

They have become so used to him as the big bad wolf of the new inquisition—technically the prefect of the Congregation for the Doctrine of the Faith—that they cannot imagine him in any other job. For some the thought is just too terrible to contemplate—that the man deemed responsible for so many of the most controversial actions of this papacy might succeed to it one day. Ratzinger has soaked up much of the odium that Catholics, still loyal at heart to their Holy Father, wish to deflect from John Paul himself. To have him as pope would be inconceivably divisive, runs the common wisdom. Besides, people say, clutching at straws, he is too old.

Oddly, the only source of encouragement for a Ratzinger papacy seemed to be the bookies. Two days after John Paul II died, one of the most popular Internet gambling sites, Paddypower.com, showed Ratzinger as a 7–1 favorite. By the time of the conclave, he ranked just after Arinze at 11–1 in what became the biggest nonsports event in the site's history. No one else seemed to be taking Ratzinger as seriously.

What many outside the Vatican had failed to notice, however, were the subterranean currents working in Ratzinger's favor. Despite his age and declining health, John Paul II had labored in the last years of his life to appoint many new cardinals. By the time of his death, all but two of the 117 voting cardinals were his appointees. They were therefore conservative and eager to extend their benefactor's legacy.

In addition, many of the most liberal cardinals were past the voting age limit of eighty. By the time of the conclave, only Carlo Martini remained to speak for the liberal perspective and even he had been declining in influence. In 2002, the pope had sent the ailing Martini to Jerusalem to pursue his love of biblical scholarship. This removed him from his power base in Milan. By contrast, the pope kept Ratzinger in Rome and as head of the powerful Congregation for the Doctrine of the Faith. The cardinals of the world took note.

Then there was the apparent transformation in Ratzinger's personal style. By all accounts, he could be painfully dry, both personally and in public. One cardinal feared that the banner over a Ratzinger papacy would be "The Bland leading the bland." Ratzinger and his supporters understood this and worked to make a change. At a funeral in Milan just weeks before John Paul II's death, both the popular Tettamanzi and the usually tepid Ratzinger spoke. In a passionate and inspiring eulogy given without notes, Ratzinger so moved the crowd that they burst into applause when he finished. Tettamanzi was forced to follow him, but his uncharacteristically plodding talk, which was read from apparently disorganized notes, met only with stony silence.

The Ratzinger makeover continued. His sermons improved and his newfound ease with a crowd was widely acknowledged. He seemed to be everywhere. He not only gave the Good Friday homily as John Paul lay dying but he also spoke at the first of the *novemdiales* Masses, at the cardinals' daily congregation meetings, and at the pre-conclave Mass, where he seemed to outline a direction for the future of the Church.

"We are moving," he declared just prior to the April 18 conclave, toward "a dictatorship of relativism . . . that recognizes nothing definite and leaves only one's own ego and one's own desires as the final measure." The modern world, he insisted, has jumped "from one extreme to the other: from Marxism to liberalism, up to libertinism; from collectivism to radical individualism; from atheism to a vague religious mysticism; from agnosticism to syncretism and on and on."[2] His answer to this disturbing scenario? A confident Church storming the future with a firm grasp on both her traditions and her times.

Many saw this as Ratzinger's bid for office. What the

world could not have known was that he had sounded exactly the tone that the cardinals needed to hear. Just days before, a ten-page document on global priestly misconduct had circulated through the Vatican. "After reading it, I was scared my heart would stop," an anonymous cardinal reported to the *Agence France-Presse*. The document underlined a "lack of coherence" of many prelates and gave examples of sexual and financial misconduct among priests as well as violations of the secrecy of the confessional.

Many cardinals were near despair. Ratzinger understood and decided to use his pre-conclave speech to show himself as the leader the Church clearly needed. "How much filth there is in the Church," he scolded, "and even among those who, in the priesthood, ought to belong entirely to Him. How much pride, how much self-complacency."[3] Ratzinger then called the Church to fresh holiness, passion for truth, and love for mankind. Vatican sources later told the Italian paper *La Stampa* that "his appeals had a profound impact on his fellow cardinals." Some even reported that a first head count of Ratzinger supporters was made immediately after the homily.

As the cardinals went into conclave later that day, the world began learning the lore of papal elections. The cardinals would meet in seclusion. Until their choice was made, their sole communication with the outside world would be the smoke that rose over Vatican City when ballots were burned after each vote: black smoke meant no decision, white meant it was time to announce "*Habamus Papam*"—"We have a pope!"

The cardinals gathered in the Sistine Chapel under the awe-inspiring work of Michelangelo. In his will, John Paul II had urged the cardinals to contemplate the lessons of the masterpiece as they went about their task. When the time came to vote, each ballot would already be printed with the words "*Eligo in Summum Pontificem*"—"I elect as Supreme Pontiff . . ." To maintain the secrecy of their ballots, the cardinals were urged to disguise their handwriting.

Having written the name of their candidate and folded their ballot twice, the cardinals would then advance one by one to an altar, hold the ballot in the air, and pronounce the oath: "I call as my witness Christ the Lord, who will be my judge that my vote is given to the one whom before God I think should be elected." Each cardinal would then place the ballot on a paten and tip it into the chalice on the altar. The ballots were then counted, announced, and burned.

Though cardinals are bound on threat of excommunication to keep the conclave proceedings secret, details of the conclave of April 18 did leak out. Most cardinals had not thought Ratzinger the lead candidate before they arrived in Rome. His media appearances, erudite homilies, and growing popular appeal made him the man to beat as the conclave convened, however. As one cardinal reported to *Time* magazine, "It's not that he wanted the job. He didn't, but his brother Cardinals saw him leading an important Mass. Watching him, there was something that had changed, almost like he had already ascended to a new level."[4]

Cardinal Martini, who had returned to Rome from Jerusalem, tried to organize liberal opposition to Ratzinger. He didn't see himself as a candidate but did want to slow Ratzinger's momentum so that other, less conservative figures could gather speed. On the first ballot, Ratzinger was clearly in the lead with Martini showing respectable support and the rest of the voting spread among various Italian candidates. Two cardinals left their ballots blank.

Analysts had said before the conclave that the twenty eligible Italian cardinals formed the bloc to watch. They could elect an Italian pope or sway the election in any way they chose. Yet not long after the conclave convened, it became clear that the Italians were not voting as a bloc. Nearly half had already declared for Ratzinger. The same was true of the entire twenty-member Latin American bloc, who were in solidarity with Ratzinger's traditional views.

On Tuesday, the second day of the conclave, Martini withdrew from contention. Liberals desperate to stop Ratzinger threw their support to Jorge Bergoglio of Buenos Aires, not even knowing that he was, according to insiders, already aligned with Ratzinger. By the second ballot, Ratzinger had sixty votes, still short of the seventy-seven required. His momentum was undeniable, though, and by the fourth ballot late on April 19 he had won 95 out of 115, an overwhelming affirmation.

Cardinal Murphy-O'Connor glanced at Ratzinger as

the direction of the voting seemed certain and noticed that "he had his head down. He must have been saying a prayer." Later Ratzinger would insist he had prayed, "Lord, please don't do this to me."[5] Nevertheless, when he was asked what name he would assume, he did not wait for the traditional ten minutes or so to pass, as though the idea of being pope had never occurred to him. Immediately, he responded with "Benedict XVI." "This was refreshing," one cardinal later told a television newscast. "He wasn't going to play the blushing bride when he had already known for some time he might be chosen."

When he was announced as the new pope from the balcony of the basilica, St. Peter's Square erupted. Joseph Ratzinger, now Benedict XVI, stepped forward and began waving joyously in answer to the roaring crowd below. An American cardinal, Chicago's Francis George, watched nearby and later said, "You know, we believe grace comes with the office. When he came out on the balcony and started waving his arms, I thought, 'It's working! I've never seen him make those gestures before!'"[6]

Then came the first public words of the new pope. "Dear brothers and sisters," he said, "after the great Pope John Paul II, the cardinals have elected me—a simple, humble worker in the vineyard of the Lord. The fact that the Lord can work and act even with insufficient means consoles me, and above all I entrust myself to your prayers. I entrust myself to your prayers." The ecstatic masses immediately began chanting: "Benedict, Benedict!"

Within minutes, the world became obsessed with the story of the quiet German scholar who had become pope. That he had been a member of the Hitler Youth was of concern to some. That he had led the CDF so aggressively against dissent within Catholic ranks was of concern to even more. Others, though, were more fascinated with his love of cats, the piano, and Bavarian beer. His work ethic was also publicly touted by Vatican insiders: that he would write for twelve hours at a time without eating or dictate twenty pages to his secretary without error. Reporters loved to describe how he struggled with modern technology: he had never driven a car, was intimidated by a computer, and was known to have disagreements with his toaster.

Ratzinger tales poured into press rooms the world over. Bavarians weighed in with recollections of the time he accepted an off-the-cuff invitation to dinner from a woman selling asparagus by the side of the road. The cardinal soon found himself seated at a simple family meal with children scampering at his feet—and having a joyous time. A hospital administrator in India reported mailing an appeal for financial help and receiving in return a personal check for twenty thousand German marks from Joseph Ratzinger. When the administrator expressed his gratitude, the cardinal replied, "Dear Rev. father, by sending you a small help I have only fulfilled my Christian obligation."

Some of the tales that made the rounds bordered on the absurd. According to one such story—which later proved true—the Golden Palace Casino in Austin, Texas, purchased a Volkswagen Golf on eBay that was supposed to have once belonged to Cardinal Ratzinger. The casino purchased the car for some $244,000 in an auction that drew eighty-four million visitors to eBay in ten days. EBay is the same Web site that had also offered for sale a grilled cheese sandwich bearing an image of the Virgin Mary and a piece of chicken that resembled John Paul II. The Vatican said only that Ratzinger had never held a driver's license and therefore could not have driven the car.

Yet the story that must have touched the new pope's heart most was of his own brother coming to his defense. Georg, then an elderly priest of eighty, had heard enough speculation about his brother's Nazi past. Breaking a long-standing refusal to be bothered with the press, he did what older brothers often do and came to Joseph's defense. "Rubbish!" he said when asked about his brother's Nazi ties. "Anybody who writes such a thing must need something to write and anyone who writes that . . . doesn't understand the times as they were." Warming to his topic, Georg insisted, "He [Joseph] had no choice. You had to join or you were shot. It was a brutal regime. It was an inhuman dictatorship." When Georg's words were reported around the world, the stir over Joseph Ratzinger's involvement in the Hitler Youth died down and the elderly priest, having stood in defense of his younger brother, went back into seclusion.[7]

The Vatican's meager dispensing of news about the new pope did little to answer the world demand for information. Many of the official statements dealt with trivial matters. There was an announcement that Benedict XVI had asked that a piano be put in the papal apartments. This prompted comparison with John Paul II's installation of a swimming pool during his first months in office. There were also official comments about the global race to find Ratzinger books and how Ratzinger was even outselling

Harry Potter in some markets. Most of the Vatican announcements, though, provided little of the background and perspective on Ratzinger's life that the public demanded. Even the official biography of the new pope posted on the Vatican Web site two weeks after his election was less than forthcoming. Obviously taken from an academic introduction that Ratzinger had written himself, the first line read, "I was born in 1927 in Marktl, in Upper Bavaria." The second line of the biography was, "I did my philosophical and theological studies immediately after the war, from 1946 to 1951." The description went on to depict Ratzinger's academic life with no mention of parents, siblings, childhood, Bavaria, personal habits, or any of the anecdotes that might have endeared the new pope to an eager public.

Most of what the public learned about Benedict XVI came from his sermons and public statements. He intended to extend the legacy of John Paul II, he said. He would fight against abortion, hold the line against homosexuality in the Church, prevent the ordination of female priests, and deal firmly with the kind of scandalous behavior among priests that had marked the Church in recent years. He also intended, he said, to put John Paul II on the "fast track" to sainthood. It was a move guaranteed to find favor among those who had so passionately grieved the loss of the previous pope.

Most revealing of all, though, were the statements that amounted to a call for a new day of Catholic evangelism. At an ordination service for twenty-one new priests, for example, Benedict XVI stated that the Church's mission to the world "must continuously put us into motion, make us restless, to bring to those who suffer, to those who are in doubt, and even to those who are reluctant, the joy of Christ."[8] It may well be that he was speaking of a restlessness of his own. He had loved his Church since he was five and first saw the inspiring figure of Cardinal Faulhaber in a Bavarian village. He had deepened in that love when he found his Church a haven during the Nazi horrors and later a bulwark against the erosions of the modernist tide. Now, he was her leader. Now, he walked in the shoes of the great popes of the past—in the path pioneered by the Benedicts whose name he had made his own. Now, he would win an indifferent world to the faith he loved with his life.

EPILOGUE

Quo Vadis?

It might be myth and it might be hoax, but it has played heavily in the popular Catholic imagination and so is worth mentioning in connection to the papacy of Benedict XVI. It all began when an Irish primate named Malachy handed a series of prophetic visions to Pope Innocent II in AD 1140. They amounted, more or less, to a list of slogans but they were supposed to be descriptive of each papacy yet to come in history.

They are difficult to define. Even the *Catholic Encyclopedia* calls the slogans "mystical titles" and then hedgingly offers that "those who have undertaken to interpret and explain these symbolical prophecies have succeeded in discovering some trait, allusion, point, or similitude in their application to the individual popes, either as to their country, their name, their coat of arms or insignia, their birthplace, their talent or learning, the title of their cardinalate, the dignities which they held, et cetera."

The problem is that the mottoes are brief and their allusions are tenuous. Still, there does appear to be some substance to them. Pope John Paul II's motto according to Malachy's prophecy was *De labore solis*, "of the Sun's labor." The connection? The pope was born under a solar eclipse on May 18, 1920. John Paul I's motto was *De medietate lunae*, "in the middle of the month." He was not only born in the diocese of Belluno, which means "beautiful moon," but served as pope for less than a month.

So what of the motto of Joseph Ratzinger? Malachy attributed to his papacy the words *Gloria olivae*, "The glory of the olive." Though there are many possible interpretations, there has long been a tradition—encouraged by the fact that the man who made the prophecies public was a Benedictine—that the *Gloria olivae* papacy would belong to a member of the Order of St. Benedict who would lead the Catholic Church in a final conflict with evil before the last days. Indeed, the papacy of Benedict XVI, according to Malachy, will be the last in history. Following his mention, the prophecy concludes with these ominous words:

> In the final persecution of the Holy Roman Church, there will reign Peter the Roman, who will feed his flock among many tribulations, after which the seven-hilled city [Rome] will be destroyed and the dreadful Judge will judge the people. The end.

Since it is difficult to imagine that the elderly Ratzinger, whom many expect to be a transitional figure, could be the leader Malachy describes, there may be another interpretation of the prophecy. A Catholic priest—who was interviewed for this book but who asked not to be named—suggested,

> Perhaps the tribulation Malachy described is for a later time and the focus of Benedict XVI's term will be peace, signified by the "glory of the olive." Maybe he will offer the olive branch to the disaffected within the Church while he works for peace in the world. God, I hope so. My Church does so desperately need to heal.

It is certain that Joseph Ratzinger is familiar with one of the most oft-recited Benedictine sayings: *Succisa virescit*. The words mean "pruned, it grows again" and it is good that the new pope knows them because they may well become the banner over his term in office.

There can be no doubt: his Church is indeed being pruned. In 2004, the number of new priests in the Catholic stronghold of Dublin, Ireland, sent shock waves through the Vatican. There was only one. The news from America was almost as bleak. A recent study by author Kenneth C. Jones called *Leading Catholic Indicators: The Church Since Vatican II* told the tale. By 2020, there will be only 31,000 priests in America and half of them will be over seventy. This is down from more than 58,000 just after Vatican II.

Though it is wise to remember Mark Twain's dictum that there are three kinds of falsehoods—"lies, damn lies, and statistics"—none of the numbers that describe trends in American Catholicism bode well. More than three thousand parishes have no priests to serve them. Two-thirds of the six hundred seminaries that were operating in 1965 have now closed. The number of teaching nuns in the United States has declined by 94 percent since Vatican II. Priests studying for ordination in religious orders have dropped by more than two-thirds, the candidates for the Christian Brothers order alone declining from 912 in 1965 to only seven now. The number of Catholic high schools, the number of students in those schools, and the number of students in parochial schools has each dropped by half in the last forty years.

The statistics are equally dire for the attitudes of American Catholics toward the teachings of their Church. Catholic marriages have decreased by half, but annulments have risen from 338 to more than 50,000 since 1965. The vast majority of Catholics in America do not attend Mass regularly, believe it is possible to have an abortion and still be a good Catholic, and believe that the Eucharist is merely a symbol rather than a repeated sacrifice of the real body of Christ as Church doctrine maintains. Undoubtedly, the Vatican thanks God that America is *not* the world, and that Catholicism is thriving in Africa and South America despite losses in the West.

Yet the Church faces challenges worldwide. Financial crises top the list. The Vatican spent more than it took in

for twenty-three years until new policies requiring dioceses around the world to help carry the load reversed the
trend as of 1993. A season of prosperity followed. In the last
years of John Paul II's reign, however, the Church was back
in the red. Vatican officials blamed the declining dollar
and the cost of John Paul II's diplomatic ventures.

The clergy sex-abuse scandals were also a cause of financial trouble. In the United States alone, the payout to
victims of sex abuse has been over $840 million since 1950.
Some dioceses in the States—Spokane, Portland, and
Tucson among them—have even been forced to declare
bankruptcy. The financial damage to the Church worldwide has not only been the cost of legal action against it but
also the revenue withheld by the faithful who were reticent
to give to a Church that no longer held their confidence.[1]

It is this Church that Joseph Ratzinger now leads. He
stands in the glare of heightened world attention, a spotlight won for him by the engaging John Paul II. He leads a
Church in which officials still speak of a "Catholic spring
in the world" and yet which is beleaguered on most every
side. Now, he is the Vicar of Christ, the Chief Priest of
Roman Catholicism, the voice of God to millions.

Which way will he lead? How will he answer the question put to the apostle whose office he seeks to fill, the words of Jesus to Peter at the outskirts of Rome: Quo vadis?—"Which way are you going?"

It is, of course, too early to know. What is certain is that Joseph Ratzinger as Benedict XVI will see himself as a guardian of traditions gathered through the centuries. He will not bow the knee to the modern, nor will he yield to reforming pressures from within his Church. He has protected the borders of the faith for too many years.

There is, however, an eagerness to win over the world to what he describes as "the beauty of truth, the joy of faith." It is likely that he will push himself to be more shepherd than scholar in hopes of winning Europe, reclaiming America, and inspiring the faith in the burgeoning Catholic realms of Asia, Africa, and South America. Certainly, he knows that he is not telegenic and that he is not the charmer his predecessor was. But he will use his quick mind and his humble manner to compensate for his shyness and his lack of popular appeal. In the time that his God gives him in office, he will try to make his mark by extending both the faith as he understands it and the legacy of John Paul II into a religiously suspicious modern world.

As he does, the defining image of his life will be Bavaria. He will remember the village liturgies, the sacred dramas and the mystic faith of his youth, and he will hope to see them fill the world. He will remember, too, the suffocating evils of Nazism and he will view modern evils in the same terms. Yet he will believe, as he always has, that Holy Mother Church is both refuge and answer now as she was during his youth. He will be willing, then, for her to be pruned—by either apostasy or the sharp sword of orthodoxy—if she will rise again to greatness. This, indeed, may be the strategy of Benedict XVI, for as he has often said,

> The essential things in history begin always with the small, more convinced communities. So the Church begins with the twelve Apostles. . . . Smaller numbers, I think, but from these small numbers we will have a radiation of joy in the world.[2]

APPENDIX:

Pope Benedict XVI
in His Own Words

TRUTH

"Truth is not determined by a majority vote."
—*April 1998 Zenit.org article*

"Meaning that is self-made is in the last analysis no meaning. Meaning, that is, the ground on which our existence as a totality can stand and live, cannot be made but only received."
—*July 2000 Zenit.org article*

"We must resist the waves of today's fashions or the latest novelties. Instead, we must stand on the unerring, unchanging truth."
—*April 1998 Zenit.org article*

APPENDIX

"Unlimited trust should only be placed in the real Word of the Revelation that we encounter in the faith transmitted by the Church."
—*April 1998 Zenit.org article*

"We do not seek a Christ whom we have invented, for only in the real communion of the Church do we encounter the real Christ."
—*1996* Communio *article*

"Only reason that remains open to God, a reason that does not relegate morality to the subjective sphere and doesn't reduce it to pure calculation, can avoid the manipulation of the notion of God and the sicknesses of religion and can offer a therapy."
—*June 4, 2004, Address for the 60th anniversary of the Normandy invasion*

"Man is not trapped in a hall of mirrors of interpretations; one can and must seek a breakthrough to what is really true; man must ask who he really is and what he is to do; he must ask whether there is a God; who God is, and what the world is. The one who no longer poses these questions is by that very fact bereft of any standard or path."
—*February 13, 1999 lecture at St. Patrick's Seminary*

APPENDIX

RELATIVISM

"Having a clear faith, based on the creed of the Church, is often labeled today as a fundamentalism. . . . Whereas relativism, which is letting oneself be tossed and 'swept along by every wind of teaching,' looks like the only attitude acceptable to today's standards."
—*Homily introducing the 2005 conclave, April 18, Rome*

"We are moving toward a dictatorship of relativism which does not recognize anything as for certain and which has as its highest goal one's own ego and one's own desires."
—*Homily introducing the 2005 conclave, April 18, Rome*

THE PAPACY

"The pope must not proclaim his own ideas, but ever link himself and the Church to obedience to the Word of God, when faced with all attempts of adaptation or of watering down, as with all opportunism."
—*Homily at the Basilica of St. John in Lateran, Rome, May 7, 2005*

"The pope isn't an absolute sovereign, whose thoughts and desires are law. On the contrary, the ministry of the pope is the guarantor of the obedience toward Christ and His Word.⁵
—*Homily at the Basilica of St. John in Lateran, Rome, May 7, 2005*

"And now, at this moment, weak servant of God that I am, I must assume this enormous task, which truly exceeds all human capacity."

—*Inaugural homily at St. Peter's Square, Rome, April 24, 2005*

"I too . . . want to affirm with decisive willingness to follow in the commitment of carrying out the Second Vatican Council, in the wake of my predecessors and in faithful continuity with the two-thousand-year-old tradition of the Church."

—*Homily during the funeral of Pope John Paul II, April 8, 2005*

"Peter's current successor takes as his primary task that of working—sparing no energies—to reconstitute the full and visible unity of all Christ's followers. This is his ambition, this is his pressing duty. He is aware that showing good sentiments is not enough for this. Concrete acts that enter souls and move consciences are needed."

—*Homily during the funeral of Pope John Paul II, April 8, 2005*

SANCTITY OF LIFE

"When faced with erroneous interpretations of freedom, a pope must underline, in an unequivocal way, the inviolability of human beings, the inviolability of human life from conception to natural death."

—*Homily at the Basilica of St. John in Lateran, Rome, May 7, 2005*

"Freedom to kill is not a true freedom but a tyranny that reduces the human being into slavery."
—*Homily at the Basilica of St. John in Lateran, Rome, May 7, 2005*

FREEDOM

"If God's image becomes something partial to the point of identifying the absolute of God with a concrete community or with certain of its interests, it destroys law and morality. In this context, the good is what is at the service of my power and the difference between good and evil is blurred. Morality and law become partisan."
—*June 4, 2004, Address for the 60th anniversary of the Normandy invasion*

"There is a pathology of reason totally separated from God. We have seen it in totalitarian ideologies that denied all relationship with God and attempted to construct the new man, the new world. It always ends in horrors."
—*June 4, 2004, Address for the 60th anniversary of the Normandy invasion*

"What do we actually mean when we extol freedom and place it at the pinnacle of our scale of values? I believe that the content which people generally associate with the demand for freedom is very aptly explained in the words of a certain passage of Karl Marx in which he expresses his own dream of freedom. The state of the future Communist society will make it possible, he says, 'to do one thing today and another tomorrow; to hunt in the morning, fish in the afternoon, breed cattle in the evening and criticize after dinner, just as I please. . . .' This is exactly the sense in which average opinion spontaneously understands freedom: as the right and the opportunity to do just what we wish and not to have to do anything which we do not wish to do. Said in other terms: freedom would mean that our own will is the sole norm of our action and that the will not only can desire anything but also has the chance to carry out its desire. At this point, however, questions begin to arise: how free is the will after all? And how reasonable is it? Is an unreasonable will truly a free will? Is an unreasonable freedom truly freedom? Is it really a good? In order to prevent the tyranny of unreason must we not complete the definition of freedom as the capacity to will and to do what we will by placing it in the context of reason, of the totality of man? And will not the interplay between reason and will also involve the search for the common reason shared by all men and thus for the compatibility of liberties? It is obvious that the question of truth is implicit in the question of the reasonableness of the will and of the will's link with reason."

—*Spring 1996* Communio *article*

THE CHURCH

"Grant that we may be one flock and one shepherd. . . . Do not allow your net to be torn. Help us to be servants of unity!"

—*Inaugural homily at St. Peter's Square, Rome, April 24, 2005*

"The communion of saints consists not only of the great men and women who went before us and whose names we know. All of us belong to the communion of saints, we who have been baptized in the name of the Father, and of the Son and of the Holy Spirit, we who draw life from the gift of Christ's body and blood, through which he transforms us and makes us like himself. Yes, the Church is alive—this is the wonderful experience of these days. During those sad days of the pope's illness and death, it became wonderfully evident to us that the Church is alive. And the Church is young. She holds within herself the future of the world and therefore shows each of us the way towards the future. The Church is alive and we are seeing it: we are experiencing the joy that the Risen Lord promised his followers. The Church is alive—she is alive because Christ is alive, because he is truly risen. In the suffering that we saw on the Holy Father's face in those days of Easter, we contemplated the mystery of Christ's passion and we touched his wounds. But throughout these days we have also been able, in a profound sense, to touch the Risen One. We have been able to experience the joy that he promised, after a brief period of darkness, as the fruit of his resurrection."
—*Inaugural homily at St. Peter's Square, Rome, April 24, 2005*

HOLINESS

"Heroic virtue does not mean that the saint performs a type of 'gymnastics' of holiness, something that normal people do not dare to do. It means rather that in the life of a person God's presence is revealed—something man could not do by himself and through himself. Perhaps in the final analysis we are rather dealing with a question of terminology, because the adjective 'heroic' has been badly interpreted. Heroic virtue properly speaking does not mean that one has done great things by oneself, but rather that in one's life there appear realities which the person has not done himself, because he has been transparent and ready for the work of God."

—*October 6, 2002, article on the canonization of Josemaría Escrivá de Belaguer*

"To be a saint is nothing other than to speak with God as a friend speaks with a friend. This is holiness."

—*October 6, 2002, article on the canonization of Josemaría Escrivá de Belaguer*

THE MEANING OF LIFE

"The deepest poverty is the inability of joy, the tediousness of a life considered absurd and contradictory. This poverty is widespread today, in very different forms in the materially rich as well as the poor countries. The inability of joy presupposes and produces the inability to love, produces jealousy, avarice—all defects that devastate the life of individuals and of the world."

—*December 12, 2000, address to catechists and teachers*

"Human life cannot be realized by itself. Our life is an open question, an incomplete project, still to be brought to fruition and realized. Each man's fundamental question is: How will this be realized—becoming man? How does one learn the art of living? Which is the path toward happiness? To evangelize means: to show this path—to teach the art of living."

—*December 12, 2000, address to catechists and teachers*

"'We are living in alienation, in the salt waters of suffering and death, in a sea of darkness without light,' he said. 'The net of the Gospel pulls us out of the waters of death and brings us into the splendor of God's light, into true life. The modern world is . . . a spiritual and emotional desert of poverty, abandonment, loneliness . . . and destroyed love.'"

—*2001 Zenit.org article*

JOHN PAUL II

"We can be sure our beloved pope is standing today at the window of the father's house, that he sees us and blesses us."

—*Homily during the funeral of Pope John Paul II, April 8, 2005*

"Today we bury his remains in the earth as a seed of immortality. Our hearts are full of sadness, yet at the same time [full] of joyful hope and profound gratitude."

—*Homily during the funeral of Pope John Paul II, April 8, 2005*

APPENDIX

"The death of the Holy Father John Paul II and the days that followed have been an extraordinary moment of grace for the Church and the whole world. The great pain for his loss and the sense of void that he left in everybody have been softened by the action of the risen Christ, which showed over long days in the coral wave of faith, love and spiritual solidarity, which peaked in his solemn funeral rites."

—*Homily during the funeral of Pope John Paul II, April 8, 2005*

"We can say it: John Paul II's funeral has been a truly extraordinary experience in which the power of God was somehow perceived."

—*Homily during the funeral of Pope John Paul II, April 8, 2005*

"I seem to feel his strong hand holding mine, I feel I can see his smiling eyes and hear his words, at this moment particularly directed at me: 'Be not afraid.'"

—*Homily during the funeral of Pope John Paul II, April 8, 2005*

"I am thinking especially about the youths. My affectionate thought goes to them, Pope John Paul II's privileged interlocutors, while, God willing, I wait to meet with them in Cologne on the occasion of the next World Youth Day. I will continue the dialogue with you, dear youths, future and hope of the Church and mankind."

—*2005 Zenit.org article*

APPENDIX

OTHER FAITHS

"In the wake of his predecessors, he is fully determined to cultivate any initiative that might seem appropriate to promote contacts and understanding with representatives of different churches and ecclesial communities."
—*Homily during the funeral of Pope John Paul II, April 8, 2005*

"I address everybody, even those who follow other religions or who simply look for an answer to life's fundamental questions and still haven't found it. To all, I turn with simplicity and affection, to ensure that the Church wants to continue weaving an open and sincere dialogue with them, in the quest for the real good for man and society."
—*2005 Zenit.org article*

"I will spare no efforts and dedication to continue the promising dialogue with different civilizations that was started by my cherished predecessors, so that a better future for everybody originates from mutual comprehension."
—*2005 Zenit.org article*

"If it is true that the followers of other religions can receive divine grace, it is also certain that objectively speaking they are in a gravely deficient situation in comparison with those who, in the church, have the fullness of the means of salvation."
—Dominus Iesus *decree, Congregation for the Doctrine of the Faith, 2000*

APPENDIX

"It is true that the Muslim world is not totally mistaken when it reproaches the West of Christian tradition of moral decadence and the manipulation of human life. . . . Islam has also had moments of great splendor and decadence in the course of its history."
—*March 6, 2002, Zenit.org article*

"That the Jews are connected with God in a special way and that God does not allow that bond to fail is entirely obvious. We wait for the instant in which Israel will say yes to Christ, but we know that it has a special mission in history now . . . which is significant for the world."
—*Joseph Cardinal Ratzinger and Peter Seewald*, God and the World

"Our Christian conviction is that Christ is also the messiah of Israel. Certainly it is in the hands of God how and when the unification of Jews and Christians into the people of God will take place."
—God and the World

CONTEMPORARY CHALLENGES AND ISSUES

The fact that the Church is convinced of not having the right to confer priestly ordination on women is now considered by some as irreconcilable with the European Constitution."
—*April 11, 2005, Zenit.org article*

APPENDIX

"In the Church, priests also are sinners. But I am personally convinced that the constant presence in the press of the sins of Catholic priests, especially in the United States, is a planned campaign, as the percentage of these offenses among priests is not higher than in other categories, and perhaps it is even lower."
—*December 3, 2002 Zenit.org article*

"In the United States, there is constant news on this topic, but less than 1 percent of priests are guilty of acts of this type. The constant presence of these news items does not correspond to the objectivity of the information nor to the statistical objectivity of the facts."
—*December 3, 2002 Zenit.org article*

"We have such difficulty understanding this renunciation today because the relationship to marriage and children has clearly shifted. To have to die without children was once synonymous with a useless life: The echoes of my own life die away, and I am completely dead. If I have children, then I continue to live in them; it's a sort of immortality through posterity."
—*Joseph Cardinal Ratzinger and Peter Seewald,* Salt of the Earth

"The renunciation of marriage and family is thus to be understood in terms of this vision: I renounce what, humanly speaking, is not only the most normal but also the most important thing. I forgo bringing forth further life on the tree of life, and I live in the faith that my land is really God—and so I make it easier for others, also, to be-

lieve that there is a kingdom of heaven. I bear witness to Jesus Christ,
to the Gospel, not only with words, but also with this specific mode
of existence, and I place my life in this form at his disposal."
—Salt of the Earth

"Celibacy is not a matter of compulsion. Someone is accepted as a
priest only when he does it of his own accord."
—*December 3, 2002, Zenit.org article*

"Although the particular inclination of the homosexual person is
not a sin, it is a more or less strong tendency ordered to an intrinsic moral evil, and thus the inclination itself must be seen as an ob-
jective disorder."
—*1986 Letter to Bishops*

"It is deplorable that homosexual persons have been and are the
object of violent malice in speech or in action. Such treatment
deserves condemnation from the Church's pastors wherever it
occurs. . . . The intrinsic dignity of each person must always be
respected in work, in action and in law."
—*November 19, 2004, Zenit.org article*

"Above all, we must have great respect for these people who also suffer and who want to find their own way of correct living. On the
other hand, to create a legal form of a kind of homosexual marriage,
in reality, does not help these people."
—*November 19, 2004, Zenit.org article*

CHRONOLOGY

April 16, 1927   Joseph Alois Ratzinger was born in the
                  Bavarian town of Marktl am Inn, Germany.

1939   Entered seminary at the age of twelve, the
                  same year Hitler invaded Poland.

1941   Joined Hitler Youth when membership be-
                  came mandatory.

1943   Drafted into the Nazi army and served in an
                  antiaircraft unit; deserted shortly before the
                  end of the war.

June 19, 1945	Released from the American POW camp where he had been held for a short time after the war.
1946–51	Studied philosophy and theology at the University of Munich, the higher school in Freising.
June 29, 1951	Ordained as a Roman Catholic priest. Became an associate pastor at the Parish of the Precious Blood.
1953	Received a doctorate in theology from the University of Munich.
1957–69	Taught fundamental theology and dogma at universities in Bonn, Freising, Münster, and Tübingen.
1962–65	Served as theological adviser to the Archbishop Frings of Cologne at the Second Vatican Council.
1968	Students at the University of Tübingen engaged in a Marxist-inspired revolt. This became a turning point for Ratzinger.

CHRONOLOGY

1969   Became professor and then vice president of
the University of Regensburg.

1977   Appointed archbishop of Munich and
Freising by Pope Paul VI and elevated to cardinal one month later.

1981   Called by Pope John Paul II to be prefect of
the Congregation for the Doctrine of
the Faith.

1998   Elected vice dean of the College
of Cardinals.

2002   Named dean of the College of Cardinals.

April 19, 2005 Elected pope by the College of Cardinals;
took the name Benedict XVI.

NOTES

INTRODUCTION

1. Joseph Cardinal Ratzinger, *Milestones* (San Francisco: Ignatius Press, 1998), p. 137.
2. Ibid, p. 138.
3. "Turbulence on Campus in 60's Hardened Views of Future Pope," Richard Bernstein, Daniel J. Wakin, and Mark Landler, *New York Times,* April 24, 2005.
4. *Milestones,* p. 137.
5. Ibid.
6. Ibid.
7. Scott Shepard, " '04 Ratzinger Letter Seen as Kerry Rebuke," Cox News Service, April 21, 2005.

8. Center for Applied Research in the Apostolate, Georgetown University, "Sixty-three Percent of Catholics Voted in 2004 Presidential Election," annual CARA Catholic Poll (CCP) 2004, http://cara.georgetown.edu/Press112204.pdf.

9. "Pope 'Prayed Not to Be Elected': Benedict XVI Meets Other Faith Leaders," CNN (posted April 25, 2005), www.cnn.com/2005/world/europe/04/25/pope.Monday/.

10. "Turbulence on Campus."

CHAPTER 1

1. Quoted in Aidan Nichols, *The Theology of Joseph Ratzinger* (Edinburgh: T & T Clark, 1988), pp. 5–6.

2. Mark Landler and Richard Bernstein, "Pope Benedict XVI: Recollections; A Future Pope Is Recalled: A Lover of Cats and Mozart, Dazzled by Church as a Boy," *New York Times,* April 22, 2005, p. A12.

CHAPTER 2

1. See I. Volk, *Der Bayerische Episkopat und der Nationalsozialismus 1930–1934* (Mainz, 1966), pp. 170–74.

CHAPTER 3

1. George Weigel, *Witness to Hope* (New York: Cliff Street Books, 1999), p. 244.

NOTES

2. Ibid.

3. Richard N. Ostling, "Keeper of the Straight and Narrow," *Time*, December 6, 1993, 142: 24, p. 58.

4. Thomas Cahill, *John XXIII* (New York: Penguin, 2002), pp. 147–48.

5. Ibid.

6. Helen Whitney and Jane Barnes, "John Paul II: The Millennial Pope," *Frontline*, PBS, p. 5 transcript.

7. Pope John Paul II, "Man Is a Spiritual and Corporeal Being," general audience, April 16, 1986.

8. John Cornwell, *The Pontiff in Winter* (New York: Doubleday, 2004), p. 304.

CHAPTER 4

1. J. A. Wylie, *History of Protestantism* (London, New York: Cassell, 1899), book 15, chapter 11.

2. John Elson, "*Time* Man of the Year: John Paul II," *Time*, December 26, 1994, 144: 26.

3. Interview with the author, May 5, 2005.

4. John Allen, *Cardinal Ratzinger: The Vatican's Enforcer of the Faith* (London, New York: Continuum, 2000).

5. Interview with the author, April 24, 2005.

6. Interview with the author, May 2, 2005.

CHAPTER 5

1. Dialogues of St. Gregory, introduction in Migne, P.L. LVXI. Public domain. Available at www.fordham.edu.

2. Homily of the dean of the College of Cardinals, Joseph Cardinal Ratzinger, at the Mass for the Election of the Roman Pontiff, Vatican Radio, April 18, 2005, www.oecumene.radiovaticana.org/en1/Articolo.asp?Id= 33990.
3. Ibid.
4. Jeff Israely, "The Conquest of Rome," *Time*, May 2, 2005, 165: 18, p. 34.
5. Associated Press, April 25, 2006.
6. Nancy Gibbs, "The New Shepherd," *Time*, May 2, 2005, 165: 18, p. 30.
7. Christian Spolar, "Brother Defends Pope Benedict's Youth in Hitler's Germany," *Chicago Tribune*, April 25, 2005.
8. Frances D'Emilil, "Benedict XVI Leads Ceremony to Ordain Priests," *Houston Chronicle*, May 15, 2005.

EPILOGUE

1. April 12, 2004, Associated Press story, reprinted in *Salon*, www.salon.com/news/wire/2005/04/12/pope/print.html.
2. Peter J. Boyer, "A Hard Faith," *New Yorker*, May 16, 2005.

BIBLIOGRAPHY

PRIMARY SOURCES

Bernstein, Carl, and Marco Politi. *His Holiness: John Paul II and the History of Our Time.* New York: Penguin Books, 1997.

Burke, Greg, and Pope John Paul II. *An Invitation to Joy.* New York: Simon & Schuster, 1999.

Cahill, Thomas. *Pope John XXIII (A Penguin Life).* New York: Viking Penguin, 2002.

Collins, Paul. *The Modern Inquisition: Seven Prominent Catholics and Their Struggles with the Vatican.* Woodstock, NY: Overlook Press, 2004.

Cornwell, John. *The Pontiff in Winter: Triumph and Conflict in the Reign of John Paul II.* New York: Doubleday, 2004.

BIBLIOGRAPHY

Crocker, H. W. *Triumph: The Power and the Glory of the Catholic Church, a 2,000-Year History.* Roseville, CA: Prima Publishing, 2003.

Flynn, Raymond L., Robin Moore, and Jim Vrabel. *John Paul II: A Personal Portrait of the Pope and the Man.* New York: St. Martin's Press, 2002.

Hebblethwaite, Peter, and Ludwig Kaufmann. *John Paul II: A Pictorial Biography.* Maidenhead, England: McGraw-Hill, 1979.

Journalists of Reuters. *Pope John Paul II: Reaching Out Across Borders.* Upper Saddle River, NJ: Reuters Prentice Hall, 2003.

Nichols, Aidan. *The Theology of Joseph Ratzinger: An Introductory Study.* Edinburgh, Scotland: T. & T. Clark Publishers, 1994.

O'Brien, Darcy. *The Hidden Pope: The Untold Story of a Lifelong Friendship That Is Changing the Relationship Between Catholics and Jews: The Personal Journey of John Paul II and Jerzy Kluger.* Emmaus, PA: Rodale Press, 1998.

Ratzinger, Joseph Cardinal, et al. *Church and Women: A Compendium.* San Francisco: Ignatius Press, 1988.

————. *Milestones: Memoirs, 1927–1977.* San Francisco: Ignatius Press, 1998.

————. *The Ratzinger Report.* San Francisco: Ignatius Press, 1987.

————. *Truth and Tolerance.* San Francisco: Ignatius Press, 2004.

Ratzinger, Joseph Cardinal, and Peter Seewald. *God and the World: Believing and Living in Our Time: A Conversation with Peter Seewald.* San Francisco: Ignatius Press, 2002.

Segundo, Juan Luis. *Theology and the Church: A Response to Cardinal Ratzinger.* San Francisco: Harper San Francisco, 1987.

Szulc, Tad. *Pope John Paul II.* New York: Simon & Schuster, 1996.

BIBLIOGRAPHY

Toropov, Brandon. *The Complete Idiot's Guide to the Popes and the Papacy.* Indianapolis: Alpha Books, 2001.

Weigel, George. *Witness to Hope: The Biography of Pope John Paul II.* New York: HarperCollins, 2005.

BOOKS OF INTEREST

Ratzinger, Joseph Cardinal. *Behold the Pierced One.* San Francisco: Ignatius Press, 1986.

————. *Building the Temple of God.* New York: Crossroad Publishing, 1996.

————. *Called to Communion: Understanding the Church Today.* San Francisco: Ignatius Press, 1996.

————. *Church, Ecumenism, and Politics.* New York: Crossroad Publishing, 1988.

————. *Daughter Zion: Marian Thoughts.* San Francisco: Ignatius Press, 2005.

————. *Dogma and Preaching.* Quincy, IL: Franciscan Press, 1983.

————. *Faith and the Future.* Quincy, IL: Franciscan Press, 1971.

————. *God Is Near Us.* San Francisco: Ignatius Press, 2003.

————. *God of Jesus Christ.* Quincy, IL: Franciscan Press, 1998.

————. *Gospel, Catechism and Catechesis: Sidelights on the Catechism of the Catholic Church.* San Francisco: Ignatius Press, 1997.

————. *In the Beginning . . .: A Catholic Understanding of the Story of Creation and the Fall.* Huntington, IN: Our Sunday Visitor, 1990.

BIBLIOGRAPHY

————. *International Theological Commission: Texts and Documents, 1969–1985*. San Francisco: Ignatius Press, 1989.

————. *Introduction to Christianity*. New York: Crossroad Publishing, 1970.

————. *Journey Toward Easter*. New York: Crossroad Publishing, 1987.

————. *Many Religions, One Covenant*. San Francisco: Ignatius Press, 1999.

————. *Meaning of Christian Brotherhood*. San Francisco: Ignatius Press, 1993.

————. *Nature and Mission of Theology*. San Francisco: Ignatius Press, 1995.

————. *A New Song for the Lord: Faith in Christ and Liturgy Today*. New York: Crossroad Publishing, 1995.

————. *Pilgrim Fellowship of Faith: The Church as Communion*. San Francisco: Ignatius Press, 2005.

————. *Principles of Catholic Theology: Building Stones for Fundamental Theology*. San Francisco: Ignatius Press, 1987.

————. *Seek That Which Is Above*. San Francisco: Ignatius Press, 1986.

————. *The Spirit of the Liturgy*. San Francisco: Ignatius Press, 2000.

————. *To Look on Christ: Exercises in Faith, Hope, and Love*. New York: Crossroad Publishing, 1991.

————. *Turning Point for Europe*. San Francisco: Ignatius Press, 1994.

Ratzinger, Joseph Cardinal, and Christoph Schonborn. *Introduction to the Catechism of the Catholic Church*. San Francisco: Ignatius Press, 1997.

Ratzinger, Joseph Cardinal, et al. *End of Time? The Provocation of Talking about God*. Mahwah, NJ: Paulist Press, 2005.

Ratzinger, Joseph Cardinal, and Aidan Nichols, editor. *Eschatology:*

BIBLIOGRAPHY

Death and Eternal Life. Washington, D.C.: Catholic University of America Press, 1988.

Ratzinger, Joseph Cardinal, and Victoria H. Lane. *Feast of Faith*. San Francisco: Ignatius Press, 1986.

Ratzinger, Joseph Cardinal, William May, and Albert Vanhoye. *Catholic Priest as Moral Teacher and Guide*. San Francisco: Ignatius Press, 1990.

Ratzinger, Joseph Cardinal, and Peter Seewald. *Salt of the Earth: Christianity and the Catholic Church at the End of the Millennium*. San Francisco: Ignatius Press, 1997.

ACKNOWLEDGMENTS

It was St. Pius X who once barked, "Miracles they want now! As if I didn't have enough to do." I am afraid I have driven those who worked with me on this book to much the same complaint: "Miracles he wants now! As if he hasn't already given me enough to do."

Still, they have labored valiantly. Bev Darnall and her amazing team at Chartwell Literary Group (www.chartwellliterary.com) have conducted the research, coordinated the travel, and scheduled the interviews that form the core of this book. Their skill and learning have made this a far more insightful work than I could have produced on my own. Ronn Huff, Jr., chased down rare books, wisely navigated obscure corners of the Internet, and often answered my most difficult questions within minutes. George Grant was, once again in my life, a mentor and coconspirator. He was also patient, even allowing this frantic author to disturb him on his thirtieth wedding anniversary. Finally, Steve Brallier offered both editorial honesty and theological passion of a kind that made the late-night hours at the keyboard a joy. I am grateful for each of these stalwarts and for the indispensable services of Chartwell.

During the writing of this book, I had the privilege of interviewing some of the leading spirits of Catholicism. The eminent Michael Novak was gentle with this Protestant in explaining the nuances of Roman tradition and hilarious in deploying the illustrative joke. Father Richard John Neuhaus, long a mentor to me through his writing, allowed me to look over his shoulder as he painted in brilliant colors the present "Catholic moment." Ralph Martin, director of graduate programs at Sacred Heart Seminary in Detroit and a pioneer of the Catholic Charismatic movement, took time to help me understand the hopes that rest upon Benedict XVI. And Father John Rock, who worked with Joseph Ratzinger at the Congregation for the Doctrine of the Faith, both helped me understand his faith as only a Jesuit scholar can and told better stories over a late-night dinner than I ever could. Thank you, my Catholic friends and fellow Christians, for helping me on my journey—both of literature and faith.

My own team had to carry a heavy load during the weeks that

I was absorbed in writing. Shirley Catalina handled everything from public relations to groceries and only occasionally gave me the quizzical look that warned of approaching insanity. Susan Levine loved me and got me where I needed to go, as she always does. Sam Chappell helped launch this project and then wisely left the country—but I love him for his care and his wisdom anyway. And the sharp minds and sharper pencils of my accountants, Tucker and Tucker, made sure the bills were paid and the laughs were frequent.

Finally, an author dreams of an editor and a publisher who understand who he is, take risks on him, won't put up with too much from him, and make him better despite his whining. I am graced with just such seasoned souls at Tarcher Penguin. Mitch Horowitz, my editor, is just the right combination of wisdom, toughness, and friendship. Joel Fotinos has been willing to take a risk on me several times now and, though it must surely have given him a sleepless night or two, his confidence has been inspiring. And no author could ask for more aggressive support and gracious understanding than I get from Ken Siman. Partnering with them makes me love the craft of writing all the more.

ABOUT THE AUTHOR

STEPHEN MANSFIELD is an author and lecturer who focuses on faith and the role it plays in fashioning leaders and shaping cultures. After being embedded with U.S. troops in Iraq at the end of 2004, he wrote *The Faith of the American Soldier*, a look at how religion is shaping a new generation at war. Prior to that, he wrote *The Faith of George W. Bush*, which became a *New York Times* bestseller. His other works have included studies of Winston Churchill, George Whitefield, and Booker T. Washington.

Mansfield lives in downtown Nashville, Tennessee, where he leads a research and education firm called The Mansfield Group and nurtures an addiction to books and racquetball. His Web site is www.mansfieldgroup.com.